CASTELLS AND
THE MEDIA

Theory and Media

Philip N. Howard, *Castells and the Media*
Paul A. Taylor, *Žižek and the Media*
Geoffrey Winthrop-Young, *Kittler and the Media*

CASTELLS AND THE MEDIA

PHILIP N. HOWARD

polity

The right of Philip N. Howard to be identified as Author of this Work has been asserted in accordance with the UK Copyright, Designs and Patents Act 1988.

First published in 2011 by Polity Press

Polity Press
65 Bridge Street
Cambridge CB2 1UR, UK

Polity Press
350 Main Street
Malden, MA 02148, USA

ISBN-13: 978-0-7456-5258-0
ISBN-13: 978-0-7456-5259-7(pb)

A catalogue record for this book is available from the British Library.

Typeset in 10.75 on 14 pt Janson
by Servis Filmsetting Ltd, Stockport, Cheshire
Printed and bound in Great Britain by MPG Books Group Limited, Bodmin, Cornwall

The publisher has used its best endeavours to ensure that the URLs for external websites referred to in this book are correct and active at the time of going to press. However, the publisher has no responsibility for the websites and can make no guarantee that a site will remain live or that the content is or will remain appropriate.

Every effort has been made to trace all copyright holders, but if any have been inadvertently overlooked the publisher will be pleased to include any necessary credits in any subsequent reprint or edition.

For further information on Polity, visit our website: www.politybooks.com

For Professor Castells, an inspiring social scientist

CONTENTS

FIGURES

ACKNOWLEDGMENTS

This book was inspired by a series of lectures given by Professor Manuel Castells at the University of Washington in 2010. As a visiting Walker Ames lecturer, Castells also met with students, and joined my graduate seminar for several long conversations. The grace with which he encouraged students to pursue their own lines of inquiry inspired me to find ways of making his ideas and work accessible to a broad audience. And I believe he would say that the participants in the graduate seminar, a well-read group from across the social sciences and humanities, offered constructive critiques and comments on his latest research. I am very grateful to the Simpson Center, directed by Dr Kathleen Woodward, for initiating and supporting the graduate seminar.

Even as a book, this work is a result of digital media networks. First, this book was written and edited in the cloud. It did not appear in material form, and will not appear as such, unless you buy it in material form. The file didn't even really reside on my hard drive while I was working on it; it was located on a server somewhere in the network. When software crashes or network disconnects necessitated, I used a backup file that did reside on my hard drive, but for the most part I was saving the file to the network. The research for this book was done online; the journals consulted were electronic. I have copies of Castells' books, but used digital versions of them for searching within the text and interrogating the ideas in non-linear ways.

Second, Castells' ideas need to be situated in the wider network of media researchers. This book is dedicated to Castells and is about his ideas (though I may put my interpretive spin on some things). It would make for rough reading to offer citations at every sentence, so this book is not an annotated bibliography. I provide direct citation to entry points for important themes and sources of criticism, but the goal is to interest readers in moving on to the original ideas and primary texts. Sometimes this may mean moving on to other scholars and their texts.

Figures I.1 and I.2 appear courtesy of Chris Harrison from http://chrisharrison.net/projects/internetmap/index.html. Figure 3.1 appears courtesy of Gene Keo from http://blogs.law.harvard.edu/anderkoo/2008/10/14/a-network-analysis-of-the-obama-08-campaign/. Figure 3.2 was made using the graphing tool at www.theyrule.net. Figure 4.1 is from Manuel Castells and Amelia Arsenault, "The Structure and Dynamics of Global Multi-Media Business Networks" in the *International Journal of Communication* 2 (2008), 707–748, and appears courtesy of the authors. Figure 5.1 appears courtesy of me.

For problems with this book I blame Rebecca Fahrig, Werner Colangelo, Carson Fahrig-Colangelo, Josh, Helen, Oscar and Angus Whitkin, Sandy Oh, Tracy Cassavant, Nathalie Oh-Cassavant, Gino Segre, Kate Gordon, and Julia Segre, and the other "friends" who interrupted and complicated my work. Some of the insights in this book have come through teaching, which is itself an important part of the research process. So I must gratefully acknowledge the good and bad questions that came from undergraduate students who have been part of "Basic Concepts of New Media" and the graduate students in the "Communication and Power" seminar. Muzammil Hussain assisted with the compilation of Castells' articles and book chapters, and Aiden Duffy designed the procedures for extracting Facebook data for the exercise on visualizing social networks. I am grateful for Andrea Drugan's vision as a Polity editor. I did this book for Hammer and Gordon Howard, and I mean that literally. Not in the sense that I expect them to read it, but in the sense that they are the main reason I look for additional work.

Penang, Malaysia

INTRODUCTION

Manuel Castells is one of the most important contemporary social scientists. His nicely crafted research questions have captivated many students and his findings have both inspired and provoked other scholars. His ideas about media networks and power are simultaneously among the most widely accepted and most often critiqued. Today, conversations about media, networks, and power begin with Castells' ideas.

At an intuitive level, many of us have seen significant changes in our economic, political, and cultural lives, and explaining these changes often seems to include stories about digital media. To help make sense of these distinctions that we can intuit, Manuel Castells advances a network perspective on the media, and this introductory chapter serves to outline the kinds of things that a network perspective reveals, and the kinds of things it obscures. In the final pages of this chapter I will introduce the conceptual approach of the book and outline the rest of the chapters. Throughout the book, key terms—and the definitions for these terms—are italicized in the text and repeated in a glossary at the end of the book.

A NETWORK PERSPECTIVE ON THE MEDIA

There are many analytical frames through which we can study the media, and I will argue that Castells has done much to develop one of the most prominent frames: that of the network perspective. Competing analytical frames might reveal how inequities in gender, race, ethnicity, or other forms of social inequality explain how media shape information skills, content production, or political knowledge. Other analytical frames privilege particular units of analysis, and could reveal how political actors such as nation-states or large corporations build and manipulate the power of the media. But a network perspective on the media has three fundamental assumptions.

The first assumption of a network perspective on the media is that we should do more than look at large groups and organizations as our unit of analysis. Sometimes media conglomerates, state regulators, and major political parties exert an enormous influence on and through the media. But the digital era is replete with examples of how individuals used cheap consumer electronics to have a significant impact on our political, economic, and cultural lives. Moreover, digital media artifacts themselves, such as websites and social networking applications, can be meaningful units of analysis and offer good evidence about the structure of social interaction. In this way, studying the media must involve studying large organizations that build and manage media infrastructure, the individuals who produce and consume content over media, and the content that is produced and consumed over media.

The second assumption of a network perspective on the media is that the links between units of analysis—whether organizations, individuals, or content—are more revealing than the units on their own. Understanding the media

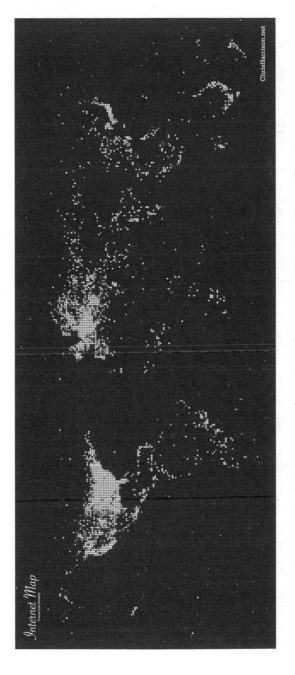

Figure I.1: Global Information Infrastructure, Glowing as Server Locations

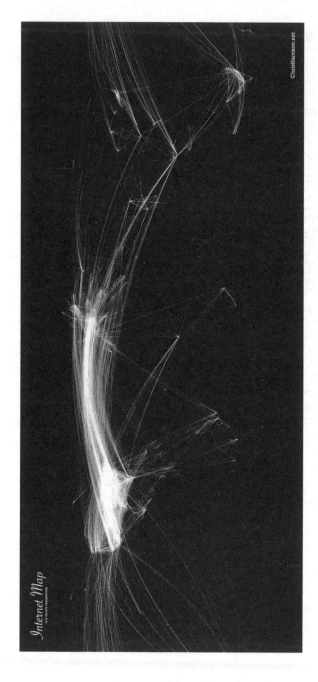

Figure I.2: Global Information Infrastructure, Glowing as Traffic between Servers

cannot come from simply cataloging the major players in a media system. It comes from understanding how governments, firms, consumers, and content relate to one another. Not all networks are equivalent, and networks are made up of other networks. These ties, transactions, and linkages between organizations, individuals, and content reveal a lot about structure. People may think they are individuals who join groups, but actually they are the nodes in networks.

The third assumption of a network perspective on the media is that the structure of a network provides both capacities and constraints on social action. The many kinds of connections between owners, regulators, and users of media can be used by members of a network, but the pattern of ties may also limit the opportunities for members of a network. This web of social relations and digital linkages can bond together similar kinds of organizations, individuals, and content. It can also provide bridges between different kinds of organizations, individuals, and content. But regardless of the unit of analysis, a network perspective on studying the media reveals the ways in which linkages provide structure.

The network perspective reveals much about the global media infrastructure. For example, Figure I.1 is a visualization of the world based on the physical location of internet servers. The wealthy cities of North America, Europe, and Japan have most of the world's internet infrastructure, so these areas glow hot in the figure. The contours of the rest of the social world are just barely there, with the coastal cities of Latin America, Africa, India and Asia visible. The media infrastructure has developed, for sensible reasons, in place with urban spaces.

Yet visualizing this information infrastructure as network linkages makes for a different kind of image. Figure I.2 takes the more meaningful network perspective, because it is based on the ties between servers. What makes the digital media of the internet important, after all, is the fact that devices are linked. The network perspective in this figure reveals several additional things about global media infrastructure. Most important, imaging the flow of traffic reveals that the digital network is not randomly distributed. The internet is not really a decentralized network. Instead, there is a clear core and periphery to global digital media. Figure I.2 tells us not just which parts of the planet have most of the server infrastructure, but tells us which places are part of a core and which are part of a periphery. Centrality in a network society is not just about being a node or being densely packed together with other important nodes, but about the distribution of links between the core and periphery. In other words, the countries of Africa and Latin America certainly have information infrastructure, but the connection between them is not as important as their connection to North America and Europe.

First, the prominence of network ties between North America and Europe becomes much more salient through a network perspective. It is not just that cities in these continents have a significant digital media infrastructure, but that the social linkages of digital traffic are most vibrant.

Second, when the global digital infrastructure is viewed by physical location of servers, the African coastline is well defined. But when viewed in terms of traffic, the contours of the continent disappear. Indeed, Africa's ties to the digital network seem tenuous; only Cape Town, Durban, and Accra are prominently linked to the global flow of information. Much of Africa, Latin America, and Central Asia disappears when their importance is weighed by traffic and network connectivity.

It is exciting to study the media, whether or not you use a network perspective such as Castells'. The media has an impact on almost all domains of social life. Moreover, it is through the media that we as individuals gain some under-standing of how the rest of society lives political, economic, and cultural lives. In many modern democracies, media infrastructure makes politics, economics, and culture pos-sible. For many people, it is the media that provides the information we need to make decisions about political can-didates on Election Day, it allows us to learn about products and services available in the market place, and it brings us the creative content produced by artists. This means that the media is also an important source of political bias and mis-information, it manipulates consumers and is cluttered with advertising, and that it produces cultural content with nasty gender and racial stereotypes, poor production values, or vapid messages.

But what counts as digital media? We might immediately think of mobile phones and Facebook pages, but what are the shared properties of these different examples? There' have been several attempts to define what it is about the new media that makes them so special, or at least different from old media. Manovich, through historical comparison to other media that appeared new at one time, arrives at five important features (Manovich 2002). First, digital media are composed of code, and therefore consist of numerical rep-resentations of material things. Second, digital media are modular, in the sense that component symbols and sounds can be creatively assembled into larger, meaningful, cultural products. Third, digital media consist of and support many automated processes. Fourth, digital media are variable, in that copies can proliferate with slight variations and result in different versions. Finally, digital media involve some cul-tural transcoding, whereby offline cultural symbols retain their meaning online, and technologies themselves become meaningful cultural symbols, perhaps indicating the wealth, sophistication, or cosmopolitanness of their users. This is certainly one of the most abstracted definitions of the new media that seem to transform the way we communicate. For Castells' purposes, it may suffice to say that the technologies that seem most transformative have two properties: they are digital and networked.

Still, when we investigate "the media" we can refer to many things: the small number of large firms that own broadcast radio and television stations, the journalists and editors who make decisions about how to present the news, the big Hollywood studios, or the information infrastructure that actually delivers content. A network perspective allows us to make important connections between who the media is and what the media is. *The media can be defined in three parts, consisting of (a) the information infrastructure and tools used to produce and distribute content, (b) the content that takes the form of personal messages, news, ideas, and cultural products, and (c) the people, organizations, and industries that produce and consume content. Using a network perspective, researching the media refers to studying the linkages and relationships between tools, content, producers, and consumers.* Castells' network perspective has allowed him to expose how digital media technologies serve power, whether for the benefit of social elites or average citizens.

OUTLINE OF THE BOOK

Castells is an important thinker because of the care he has taken to document and analyze the impact of new media technologies on social life. Not everyone agrees with his findings and conclusions. But almost everyone would agree that digital media, such as mobile phones and the internet, have had an enormous social impact. This impact has been mostly strongly felt since the mid-1990s, so the evidence presented in the chapters ahead is deliberately selected to help contrast the organization of political, economic, and cultural life before and after the diffusion of digital media. Wherever possible, a network perspective will be used to analyze the role of digital media in changing patterns in these three domains of social interaction. Other researchers contribute to the network perspective—they build on Castells' work and he builds on theirs. Since Castells is an important node in the scholarly network, I will reference some of those scholars in the chapters ahead.

The first chapter offers an intellectual biography by telling the story of his progress through the academy. This will not be exhaustive, and readers are encouraged to review Felix Stalder's excellent book *Manuel Castells: the Theory of the Network Society* for more information on Castells' intellectual development (Stalder 2006). In addition, Martin Ince leads a good intellectual conversation in *Conversations with Manuel Castells* and Ida Susser offers annotations on excerpts from Castells' writings on the informational city in *The Castells Reader on Cities and Social Theory* (Castells and Ince 2003; Susser 2002). In the opening of *Communication Power* (2009), Castells himself offers a compelling story of the journey from student radical to social scientist. The first chapter of this book proceeds from intellectual biography to a brief meta-analysis of the impact of Castells' writings on other scholars. The first chapter then concludes with a discussion of the theory of the network society as it relates to the study of media tools, content, producers, and consumers. There are other important scholars who use a network perspective to analyze social transformation. These scholars have done important work, but this is a book about Castells and his network perspective on media.

The second chapter discusses Castells' research on the economics of media, the third chapter discusses his research on networks of power and politics, and the fourth chapter discusses his research on cultural production. Chapter 5 is dedicated to using—and critiquing—Castells' insights with reference to the latest trends in mobile and social media. Every analytical frame has its strengths and weakness. Or it might be more accurate to say that every analytical frame reveals some things but obscures others. The final chapter examines some of the critiques of Castells' work on the media. The goal of this chapter will not be to discredit him or his contributions, but to identify the questions that still need to be answered. In part, this chapter is about identifying the questions that readers may be inspired to answer.

This book ends with an appendix containing three exercises that will help the reader understand the network perspective on media. These exercises will help the reader understand the personal and global contexts of their *own* networks—the structures that provide you with capacities and constraints on your future. Throughout, footnotes will be used to (1) offer citations to particular articles or book sections on particular topics that might interest the reader, or (2) offer examples of multimedia content that provides a good punch line.

1

CASTELLS AND THE THEORY OF
THE NETWORK SOCIETY

This first chapter serves to introduce Manuel Castells and the research path he has taken. While the book as a whole is titled *Castells*, most of the biographical information appears in this chapter. Since he has advanced research in multiple disciplines, this chapter will also explain the domains in which he has worked and the labels he has been given. He has taken—or been given—several kinds of monikers during a career path from as a Marxist sociologist in France, an urban geographer at UC-Berkeley, to a professor of communication with multiple institutional affiliations. Thus, this chapter will chart his course—and his contribution—to the study of media.

INTELLECTUAL BIOGRAPHY

Manuel Castells was born in Hellín, Spain, in 1942. He was raised in Barcelona and lived there until his student activism drew the wrath of the dictator Francisco Franco. Castells moved to France and earned a doctorate in Sociology from the University of Paris. His personal interest in resisting cultural power continued, and his participation in the 1968 public protests cost him his instructor's job at the Paris X University Nanterre. Subsequently, he taught at École des Hautes Études en Sciences Sociales, and in 1979 he moved to the University of California at Berkeley. There he was appointed to a joint professorship in the Department of Sociology and the Department of City and Regional Planning. In 2001 he formally joined the Open University of Catalonia as a research professor and in 2003 he accepted a position as Chair of Communication and Technology at the University of Southern California. In recent years he has split his time between researching and mentoring in Los Angeles and Barcelona. Indeed, he mentors a large network of people who study the media, technology, and power.

Initially, Castells was most interested in urban sociology, and he helped develop a Marxist approach to the study of social transformation in large cities. Social movements and civic activism played a key role, according to Castells, in the evolution of urban spaces. Public resources, such as transportation systems, housing, and libraries, brought together people of diverse backgrounds and formed the basis of collective experience in the modern city. Yet by the 1980s many of the cities he studied were also developing digital infrastructures that enabled new forms of economic exchange and political power. If cities represented the seat of power in economic development, digital networks were significantly extending the ability of urban centers to marshal distant resources and project that power farther afield. For the most part, these digital networks only served governments, media barons, and financial institutions, and they were good servants. Information technologies allowed financial actors to better evaluate the risks of their investments, estimate the return on them, and develop more complex financial instruments and trading mechanisms. These same technologies made militaries better able to project the power of the state, with satellite defense systems, smart bombs, and internal communications systems. Digital networks allowed media barons to globalize urban cultures, export media products, and customize advertising. When the internet was privatized in 1995, the digital infrastructure that had served to connect powerful institutions in global cities began to serve individuals who had access to consumer electronics.[1]

It was during this important transformation that Castells began to study the politics of information infrastructure and media.

PUBLICATIONS AND IMPACT

Castells has published over 20 books, and there are several books about him and his ideas. There are upwards of 80 articles, working papers, speeches, and sundry publications available in different electronic libraries. Google Scholar reports that 12,000 books, book chapters, and articles offer some citation to the first volume of Castells' *The Information Age* trilogy, which is called *The Rise of the Network Society*. The other two volumes, *The Politics of Identity* and *End of Millennium* are also widely referenced. This trilogy has been translated into 22 languages, and *The Internet Galaxy* has been translated into 15 languages. His recent book *Communication Power* was eagerly awaited by social scientists across media studies, sociology, political science, geography, and many other domains of inquiry in which his theories are valued. It is hard to measure his impact, but Manuel Castells is certainly one of the most cited social scientists.

While selections of writings may appear on syllabi around the world, some researchers succumb to the instinct to cite

The Rise of the Network Society only as a general, honorary link to an influential work. As a researcher, if you want to make the assumption that digital media has revolutionized social order but then move on to your specific research questions, citation to this work is necessary. It is not always easy to go through Castells' writings: the ideas are complex; some ideas seem contradictory even though his thinking has evolved; there are some obvious points of critique. But it is not possible to dismiss his contributions, and one of the goals of this book is to intrigue readers enough through an introduction to his work that they will go on to read the original material.

But where to begin? With a broad intellectual agenda and a long publishing career, what is the best way to locate the beginnings of Castells' research on media? What menu of readings would best represent his research? Castells' research on the network society really began with his study of information and labor supplies in urban areas. The "informational city," as he called it, was an important new phenomenon that challenged the assumptions of contemporary Marxist and sociological theory. To keep this book focused, however, it may be better to begin with the research he was conducting in the mid-1990s. It was at this point that he began transporting his network perspective from the informational city to broader institutional contexts. Good theories are transportable to other contexts, so it is with the publication of *The Rise of the Network Society* that we really begin to see how his unique perspectives have bearing on media. For those who might treat this book as a companion to the original material, two menus for "Castells on the Media" can be recommended.

The short menu could include one book and a couple of book chapters and articles. *The Internet Galaxy* is Castells' most accessible book (Castells 2001). Yet, *Communication Power* is his latest major book-length work and his discussion of the power of media networks is most advanced here (Castells 2009). One good article to complement *Communication Power* could be "An introduction to the Information Age" which is a succinct statement of many of the concepts developed in the trilogy. Another could be the article-length statement about his theories of media and social structure, "Materials for an exploratory theory of the network society," which was written in response to the critiques of his trilogy (Castells 1997, 2000a).

The longer menu could include *Communication Power* and selections from *The Rise of the Network Society* (Castells 2009, 1996). *The Rise of the Network Society* is a magnum opus in the sense that it has some parts that most people read and a few parts that interest specific readers. This first volume of the trilogy *The Information Age* is the most widely read, because it offers the comprehensive statement on what the social structure of the network society looks like. The second volume is dedicated to social movements and political processes, particularly in the U.S., U.K., and Europe, which demonstrate network effects. Having developed some grand ideas in the previous volumes, the third volume is the most specific in terms of presenting evidence. Castells uses the third volume to show how two significant social events—the collapse of the Soviet Union and rise of the Asian Tigers—were the result of new forces at play in the network society. Indeed, it is in this volume that he tackles the pernicious problems of social inequality in the network society.

There are certainly other combinations and permutations of articles, book chapters, and books that could make for a good menu of readings. Different disciplines would compose their own menu of Castells' writings. Geographers might be most interested in the statements on the "space of flows" found in Chapter 6 of *The Rise of the Network Society* (which is Volume I of *The Information Age: Economy, Society and Culture*) or Chapter 8 of *The Internet Galaxy*. Organizational behavior scholars, economists, and economic historians might prefer Chapters 2 or 3 of *The Rise of the Network Society*. Sociologists most often seem to build on Chapters 1, 4, and 5. Volume II of the trilogy offers detailed study of social movements, from feminism to environmentalism. For readers interested in international relations or international political economy, Volume III of the trilogy contains rich chapters on the collapse of the Soviet Union, the Asian financial crisis of the late 1980s, and global criminal networks.

Castells is an enormously influential scholar on the media, but he is also a node in a scholarly network. That is, over the course of his career, he has built on the work of others, and they have built on his. He has collaborated with other scholars and mentored his students by coauthoring articles and book chapters and edited collections. He has effectively used his own social networks to maintain ties across intellectual communities in Barcelona, Paris, San Francisco, and Los Angeles. Universities in these cities are only nodes in Castells' globally networked intellectual community.

There are a variety of strategies one could have for linking up Castells' ideas and evidence with those of other scholars. There are other prominent scholars of digital media, so it is tempting to build in citations to the extensive network of people and texts that have influenced Castells and been influenced by him in turn. Experts can read his writings and make educated guesses about the origins of some insights. It would be possible to offer citations to other scholars when I see their relevant works and ideas in his argument or think a reader might want to go to the likely source of Castells' inspiration. Given his publication record and impact, this would result in an enormous book with a lengthy bibliography. The following chapters are meant to feature his work on the media. So for the most part, citations to other scholars will be offered when Castells himself has named them as relevant to his argument. To help readers understand Castells' use of other scholarly works, many other prominent scholars are referenced throughout this book.

BASIC STATEMENTS ON NETWORK THEORY

For those of us interested in studying the media, more seems to have changed between 2000 and the present than between 1900 and 2000. In the last decade, the vast majority of people living in wealthy countries came to have easy access to the internet and the vast majority of people around the world came to have easy access to a mobile phone. More and more people are able to maintain links to family and friends even if life takes us across the country or between continents. Most of the cultural industries and news organizations that evolved in a century of movie theaters and broadcast networks had to rapidly develop digital media strategies or face bankruptcy. In most democracies, particularly in the West, a politician without some kind of digital media campaign is unelectable. In most of the rest of the world, mobile phones activate voters or protesters at sensitive political moments.

The networks that connect people may involve media such as computers, mobile phones, Wi-Fi fields and undersea trunk cables. But these networks are fundamentally social: the network of fiber optic cable that connects cities and crosses oceans was laid deliberately, to serve (wealthy) populations. The bits that flow through cyberspace are created and received by people (though sometimes indirectly).

Castells, like Marshall McLuhan and Harold Innis, firmly argues that society cannot be understood without studying media technologies. "Technology does not determine society. Nor does society script the course of technological change, since many factors, including individual inventiveness and entrepreneurialism, intervene in the process of scientific discovery, technical innovation and social applications, so the final outcome depends on a complex pattern of interaction" (Castells 1996, 5). In his study of the social impact of the internet, Castells makes some of the same observations that McLuhan made studying the impact of the television. Castells probably uses more evidence, gathered in a more systematic way, than McLuhan. Still, McLuhan eloquently suggested that systems of electric technologies connect people to a kind of social nervous system. New communication technologies seemed to be extending our global consciousness, changing our creative processes, and generating new forms of knowledge. The electronic revolution decentralized, integrated, and accelerated social interaction, and resulted in technological convergence (McLuhan and Lapham 1994).

As an economic historian, Harold Innis was one of the first to specialize in the study of how civilizations communicate (Innis 2008). He developed three core assumptions that have held up well over time, assumptions that also back Castells' work. First, Innis argued that the use of a particular communication tool defined the quality and quantity of knowledge shared in a society and preserved about that society. Second, he argued that new communication technologies allowed for new organizational forms, so that societies becoming dependent on a single medium would tend to become stagnant and inflexible. Finally, he argued that our understanding of long-dead or culturally distant societies depended on the character of their media. If these assumptions hold true, then Castells can sensibly argue that the way we generate and share knowledge will be shaped by digital media, that digital media will support new forms of economic, political, and cultural organization. Media scholars of the future will have to confirm if our impact is interpretable only through our media.

While some researchers can seem overly enthusiastic about how new technologies will revolutionize society, it can be tough to actually find many scholars who say that technology *directly causes* social change. Quite the opposite, most researchers are careful to note that media technologies and social order evolve together and shape each other. If society cannot be understood without its media technologies, does it make sense to study media technologies without their social context? (For people who study the media, the answer is no!).

An information society is a term used in contrast with agrarian or industrial society, to emphasize that the important features of contemporary economics, politics, and culture are defined by the role of information. An information society could be simply defined as a set of social relations in which data is the most important source of value, rather than capital or labor. One of the ways Castells has advanced our understanding of the media has been by demonstrating that what has changed over the last decade is that it is not just information that is important, but the very structure and organization of information.

> The provisional outcome of my research should allow us to stop using the notion of information society and replace it with the concept of network society as the specific social structural characteristic of our time. (Castells 2000b, 110)

The notion of the information society was developed to explain the growing importance of information supplies in the economy and the rising class of information workers. Many economists and political theorists have helped fill out the metaphor of the information society. Even though different scholars emphasize different features of the information society, most of them hold one attribute constant: power resides within the nation-state. Indeed one of the ways of defining an information society is to say that the state monopolizes the tools of information, a variation on the more classic definition that the state monopolizes the tools of violence.

But Castells undermines this state-centric understanding of where power lies. He builds an argument using the work of two other prominent scholars. Ulrich Beck has argued that state power is being challenged by globalization (which limits its sovereignty), market pressures for deregulation (which reduces its capacity to intervene), and declining public legitimacy (which diminishes its influence over citizens) (Beck 2006; Castells 2007). Lance Bennett has argued that the media is a well-articulated system in which, for the most part, the print journalists generate original information and break news stories, television broadcasts information to a mass audience, and radio customizes news content and provides some interaction (Bennett 1990). Since states no longer really monopolize information, Castells argues that a significant amount of economic, political, and cultural power has actually moved from the state to the media system. Moreover, it is not simply that information is an important new source of value, which defines contemporary social life. Instead of speaking of media systems, we should refer to them as media networks. There are strong new structures—networks—that support peculiar forms of social interaction, unique patterns of authority, and particular sources of power. The power to control information no longer resides exclusively with the institutions of the state; it resides in media networks. And media networks are constituted by social relations and communication technologies.

So Castells argues that in contemporary network society the power residing in media networks is stronger than that residing in states. Industrial societies certainly had communication systems, but these were mass media that did a good job of distributing messages from one to many. In the network society the communication system distributes messages and content in very different ways, with immense implications for economic, political, and cultural life.

2

MEDIA ECONOMICS AND LIFE ONLINE

New information technologies have had a significant impact on the economy. Compared to the pre-internet era, markets operate in different ways, firms behave differently, and consumers act differently. The economy, especially in the developed world, has become both information-rich and networked. This chapter introduces some of the more popular notions of permanently beta production and the long tail. Important examples of unique economic organizations in the network society include Netflix, the economy of iPhone apps, and Amazon.com. The network perspective on economic organization reveals how strong and weak ties between firms may have more of an impact on business success than hierarchical management within the firm. Moreover, the network perspective is particularly useful for understanding the modern operations of both the small internet startups and the large media, software, and video game corporations that have adapted their management practices. Even though the dot-com boom and bust was only a few years ago, the organizational innovation of many of those small firms had an immense influence on organizational behavior across the rest of the economy (Neff 2011).

Several scholars have analyzed similar trends to those that interest Castells, but come to different conclusions. Some prefer to refer to the current organization of economic, political, and cultural life as an "information society" rather than a network society. Even though there are many distinct features to the way we live now—most notably in the importance of digital media—Castells is reluctant to think of social change as stages of growth.

Karl Marx may be one of the first social scientists, in that he made arguments from large amounts of evidence, purposefully gathered. One of his most important arguments was a theory of modernization: the idea that societies pass through stages of economic growth and all societies must advance through all of the stages for there to be progress. From feudal societies came agrarian societies. Many of these became industrial societies, and some contemporary scholars argue that the most advanced industrial societies have become information societies. But Castells does not offer such a linear model for economic development:

> The shift from industrialism to informationalism is not the historical equivalent of the transition from agricultural to industrial economies, and therefore cannot be equated with the emergence of the service economy. (Aoyama and Castells 2002, 138)

Instead, Castells argues that instead of thinking of economic development as a series of stages, it should be seen as an evolution of organizational forms. For a long time, hierarchies—such as church, state, and firm—were the most efficient and effective ways of marshaling resources and solving collective action problems. Social networks existed, but were small and personal, and not very effective means of organizing for large communal endeavors. New information technologies have given the network form of organization special prominence, especially when it comes to media businesses, political campaigns, and cultural industries. These days, networks sometimes appear even more efficient and effective than hierarchies at achieving collective goals.

Certainly, information workers are an important part of the global economy. People such as scientists, engineers, designers, accountants, and media producers are classified as information workers because of their role in creating knowledge, communicating ideas, or processing information. Certainly every job involves some information management, but for particular jobs the primary skill required is the ability to create, communicate, and process information. And on the whole, across most of the advanced economies, the professional categories that have grown the most over the last 50 years are informational: managers, technicians, and clerical workers now produce a significant amount of the economic wealth.

In addition, the economic networks that connect industries around the world generate a significant amount of wealth. Finance and cultural industries (discussed in 'Transforming Cultural Industries' on pp. 57–61 below) may be local in the sense that head offices and physical assets are physically placed somewhere. And most firms and most jobs are not global, they are usually located in cities. But in the network society, a few dominant cities constitute what Castells calls a "globalized core." It is in these cities that financial markets are actually sited. Trade in goods and services may be an international exchange, but the terms of the transaction are negotiated in concentrated centers where information managers actually do the negotiations. Science and technology research, and the specialty labor required for cultural industries to thrive, is also located in these global cities. Indeed, communication networks make possible the massive exchange of international goods and services, stocks and bonds, and currencies. The daily turnover of currency markets around the world in 1998 was US$1.5 trillion, a little more than the annual gross domestic product of the United Kingdom. Today, with the underlying information infrastructure of digital networks, the figure is almost US$4 trillion.

As explained in the previous chapter, technology and social evolution are intertwined. So information technologies cannot have been distinct, independent causes of economic globalization. But they were the medium of economic globalization. Since the 1970s, the earliest digital networks were quickly put to the use of economic networks. In hindsight, these digital networks had other consequences for the way we work and the way firms do their business. One of the foundational insights—the very beginning of the network perspective—came from Mark Granovetter. In his article, "The strength of weak ties," he demonstrated how different kinds of network ties are useful for different things (Granovetter 1973). Strong ties, to people like your family members and close friends, are best for marshaling physical resources. Weak ties, to people like your classmates or professional contacts, often transcend local social and geographic boundaries. So you are more likely to be able to borrow a car or get a small loan from your strong ties, and you are more likely to hear about a new job or dating prospect from a weak tie. Either way, social ties are what makes most economic transactions work. Today, digital media are the information infrastructures that make entire economies work.

THE PERMANENTLY BETA, NETWORK ENTERPRISE

One traditional way of organizing economic production involves using a firm, with hierarchically organized staff, that does market research and offers mass-produced goods and services to customers. But the new information technologies have allowed some businesses—especially those involved in digital media—to organize themselves and relate to their customers with a network perspective. In *The Rise of the Network Society*, Castells points out that using network ties to involve customers in the process of production can offer certain efficiencies, and that many economic and organizational processes have been informationalized since the diffusion of the internet. Neff and Stark take this idea a little farther and offer an interesting metaphor for the economics of user-driven design and cycles of testing, feedback, and innovation: a system of "permanently beta" production (2004).

Formally, the network enterprise is a "specific form of enterprise whose system of means is constituted by the intersection of segments of autonomous systems of goals" (Castells 1996, 187). In other words, the network enterprise brings in revenue through different services—sometimes products—that may have little to do with each other except in that a core group of producers think their services contribute to a shared sense of purpose. Google may be a good example of a network enterprise. Even now that it has grown in size and economic clout, its success hinges on its ability to bring together very different kinds of creative units to produce a wide variety of online tools to which advertising can be appended. Search may be a core application, but the teams that produce the myriad applications available as Google services operate with their own distinct product goals. Integration between video tools, email, and search is found at Google's central node, its search portal.

Moreover, Google only removed the beta label from many of its core applications in July 2009. It did so only because the firms realized that large corporate customers might not want to commit to using its email and word-processing applications that were in beta, even if individual customers associated the beta label with ongoing development and ingenuity. Most technology and media business projects begin as network enterprises, and some—such as Google— do not shed the features of a network enterprise as they scale up in productivity.

Yet the network enterprise is not a network of enterprises. It is, as Castells describes it, "made up of bits and pieces of firms, sometimes together in a strategic alliance for a while, in a market, on a product line" (Castells 1998, 475). Indeed, it is not only dot-com firms that represent temporary, project-based teams: film crews, surgeries, criminal investigations, criminal organizations, and social movements all have features of the permanently beta organization. A network enterprise, for Castells, resides in the collaborative partnerships that link up regional production systems with extra-regional consumption systems in a pattern of exchange.

Many network enterprises, especially in the realm of digital media, have one additional feature: the process of designing goods and services is only actually completed by the user. In other words, customers are integral to the design process because they contribute some small piece of information that makes the product more valuable to more customers. Product design is completed through use (Suchman 2006). "New information technologies are not simply tools to be applied, but processes to be developed," Castells writes (Castells 1996, 31). Google's search services only have value when people use them, because their searching algorithms incorporate some measure of social value. The value of blog and twitter feeds increases with the addition of new producers and consumers of content.

FROM BRICKS AND MORTAR TO BANDWIDTH AND SERVERS

Castells' work on the media is grounded in, and developed in parallel with, research on important changes in the economy. By the 1990s there was broad consensus that the organization of information and social networks were key features of successful businesses and modern economies. Not only was the process of producing goods and delivering services increasingly dependent on information infrastructure, but economic growth itself was increasingly dependent on technological innovation. The production, distribution, trade, and consumption of all sorts of goods and services required smart managers with intelligence on market demand, data from the supply chains, and systems of quality control. Smart business leaders have always needed to know their markets, supply chains, and product quality. But overall, economic growth mostly came from putting more capital investment or more labor resources into the business. The new way of doing things, especially in the advanced economies, involved sophisticated information systems and even new classes of labor dedicated to information management. In this way, the transition to the network society had two kinds of consequences for the organization of economic life: an impact on the specific organization within many firms; and an impact on the organization of the economy as a whole.

Traditionally, many businesses were run as hierarchies: large, bounded, and vertically integrated organizations. The lines of authority within the organization were clear. Each employee only had one supervisor, and each employee could be easily replaced by another worker with a similar skill set. These kinds of organizations were great at developing a standardized production process for mass-producing goods. These organizations are sometimes called Fordist, because Henry Ford perfected a manufacturing model that organized labor—and management—in clear hierarchical relations.

As organizational forms, hierarchies and networks are good for different things. *The hierarchy is a clearly bounded organization with clear, vertical lines of authority and replaceable workers who participate in standardized processes of production.* Hierarchies are good for marshaling large amounts of resources towards specific goals determined by the chain of command: they centralize decision making and distribute tasks for execution. Military hierarchies are the best kind of organization in times of war, employee hierarchies are the best way to organize large factories, and bureaucratic hierarchies are the best way to manage the resources of entire nations. In contrast, networks distribute both decision making and tasks, but can quickly adapt and reorganize when decisions or tasks need more thought or more resources.

The economics of media have significantly evolved over the last two decades, and digital media have had a significant impact on the way business is done in other industries.

When companies increasingly link up suppliers and customers through their websites considerably limiting their direct intervention in transactions, they are an information network. When businesses-consulting firms contract their experts for specific projects, and bring them together for the duration of the project by plane, bicycle, email or videoconference, they are an information network. When multinational corporations set up their transnational production networks linking up their internally decentralized structure with hundreds of suppliers around the world, they are information networks, since production and distribution can only operate on the basis of electronically supported exchange of information. (Castells 2000b, 112)

Beginning in the 1970s, the large economies of North America and Europe experienced a significant structural change. These economies evolved from mostly generating wealth through natural resources and manufacturing to mostly generating wealth through services and information-processing activities. Other countries, such as China and India, took on the production of material goods. And the service sector within the United States and Europe also changed. It evolved from being a part of the economy where physical labor generated wealth to being a part of the economy where managing information, writing software code, and producing culture generated wealth.

THE CHANGING NATURE OF MEDIA WORK

Work in the new economy also has unique features that make a job in news media, video games, or a dot-com startup seem distinct from other labor sectors. In contrast to most manufacturing jobs, many people find that media work is relatively unstable, unreliable, and often involves part-time, temporary, or self-employment. Many media workers, from computer programmers to graphic artists and scriptwriters, work "flextime" and have other kinds of non-standard arrangements (Deuze 2007).

At the height of the dot-com boom, many workers were accepting stock options instead of competitive salaries. They invested a lot of personal time, energy, and social capital in projects that they hoped would pay off big—a kind of investment Neff calls "venture labor." Whereas the mystique of the internet startup is that a venture capitalist takes on the risk of supporting projects that may fail, she argues that individual workers often shoulder a significant amount of risk by throwing their energy into internet startups (Neff 2011). Many other agricultural, manufacturing, and service jobs involve information processing, and Castells argues the structural transformation in the economy has very immediate effects on daily work. But media work may be the best example of economic organization in a network society, both because of how labor is organized in media industries and because of the overall economic value generated by these industries.

Media work is notoriously fickle, so new opportunities come over networks. In the global networks of economic production, the places where media work is concentrated have an unsettled workforce. In New York's Silicon Alley, Boston's Route 128, and California's Silicon Valley, an unusually high proportion of the workforce is part-time, temporary, or self-employed (Neff 2011; Saxenian 1996). Recall that a key tenet of the network perspective is that not all networks are equivalent. This means that different localities can be internationally connected by particular kinds of relations. Castells offers several examples:

> For instance, Silicon Valley or Austin are part of the decisive network of information technology innovation, but not of financial networks. London, New York, and Frankfurt (but also Moscow and Buenos Aires) are key nodes of financial and business networks, but have little relevance in networks of technological innovation. (Castells 2000b, 114)

Cultural production has been similarly networked. The large video game production firms have extensive network relationships that link up an international coterie of subcontractors to head offices in Vancouver, Seattle, and San

Francisco. Given the fluidity of success and failure in media industries, media workers are more likely to find employment across these global networks of cities than they are to adapt to slightly different industries in the same city. Network economics do not just mean that firms are connected in multinational alliances of supply chains. Network economics mean that the supply of labor follows similar chains. In looking for new work, our first instinct is to send out our resume to our social network, even if that means our resume will land in human resources departments around the country or around the world. Particularly in media industries, employment opportunities and labor mobility happen through networks.

While cultural industries have been transformed as workplaces, they are also good examples of the kinds of business that have been glocalized. The notion of glocalization will be further explored in Chapter 5 ("Cosmopolitan Culture and Cultural Identity," pp. 81–85) on culture, but it is relevant here as a descriptor of how the network flows of information have an impact on business. Communication technologies "allow for the centralization of corporate activities in a given space, precisely because they can reach the whole world from the City of London and from Manhattan without losing the dense network of localized ancillary firms" (Castells 1999, 294). But the network effect has several additional consequences, Castells elaborates. The technologies that allow such centralization also permit decentralization without much loss of efficiency. "At the same time," he points out, "back offices can decentralize into the suburbs, in newly developed metropolitan areas or in some other country and be part of the same system." Thus Vancouver is a center of video game production, and Hyderabad a center of computer engineering talent.

At the height of the dot-com boom, in 1999–2000, Castells estimated that 43 percent of all jobs in the United States were essentially information-processing jobs: professional/ technical work, managerial positions, clerical, and service jobs (Aoyama and Castells 2002). By now the amount is almost certainly higher. Media work itself is no longer simply employment in public relations, advertising, movies, or radio. Such employment often meant having a specific set of tasks that had relevance for a particular print or broadcast industry. Sometimes it even meant membership in a union that would safeguard the economic interests of screenwriters, actors, directors, musicians, or television and radio artists. Today, without those safeguards, media work may be the best example of what Castells calls "self-programmable labor" (Castells 2009, 30).

If the network enterprise leverages diverse resources to complete specific projects, a key resource is the kind of labor that has flexible and adaptable skills. In many contemporary media industries, workers have the capacity to focus on assigned goals, find relevant information, recombine information into new knowledge, and apply the knowledge to advance the project. Since our information systems are ever more complex, good search skills are among the most basic and important labor assets. Employees need to be creative and willing to adapt to sudden changes in organizational forms. They must be familiar with a wide range of technologies, and be willing to learn about new technologies. Indeed, "keeping up with technology" is a key feature of most modern jobs.

In the past, the work of a television cameraman was very different from that of a film cameraman. The modern videographer must have the digital literacy to work with equipment that functions across platforms. A contemporary graphics artist is valuable—and transportable—from the video game industry to the movie industry. But even for industries that are not directly concerned with cultural production, there are consequences for patterns of work. We must be ready for the software updates that force us to adopt new technological habits.

THE DEATH OF DISTANCE AND LONG TAILS

The economic transformation in many countries has made possible the network society. Economic globalization has displaced power from the state into the media. The way we work has changed, both in terms of our daily tasks as employees and in terms of the structure of the labor economy. And new information and communication technologies have compressed social spaces and distance barriers, allowing for knowledge transmission. Castells' observations about the network economy have been reformulated and expressed in interesting ways, as several popular notions: the death of distance, the economy of the long tail, and the economy of free.

Frances Cairncross came up with a powerful phrase for describing what she saw as the crucial economic transformation in network societies—the declining impediment of physical distance (Cairncross 1997). If distance no longer determines the cost of communication, then small companies will be able to offer many of the same products and services once only offered by large businesses. Markets will become almost frictionless, with better pricing information that enhances competition, more rational use of heavy equipment, and improvements in the mobility and reach of businesses themselves. Many corporations would become loose-knit organizations, with culture and communications holding firms together. Overall, the costs of starting businesses in this new, digital economy should decline, and many firms that were once manufacturing businesses would become service providers. But digital networks not only help firms over the challenge of long supply chains, collecting information, and providing services over great distances.

Networks of networks have the interesting property of making it possible to deliver particular kinds of content directly to the small subnetworks that most value the content. This phenomenon has been popularized as the "long tail"—business models that deliver narrow goods and services can actually find their customers if they take advantage of network relations (Anderson 2008). Instead of offering only the most popular goods and services to most people, offer almost all of the goods and services to almost all of the people. This means that if a company such as Netflix can carry even the most obscure edit of the original *Star Trek* episode "Spock's Brain," there will be a few thousand U.S. adults willing to pay to rent it as a DVD.

THE NETWORK PERSPECTIVE ON ECONOMIC LIFE

Two prominent scholars echo Castells' work on the economics of cultural production, both taking a network perspective. In *Democratizing Innovation*, Eric von Hippel argues that there can be very specific circumstances in which a user community can be very effective developers of new ideas and products (von Hippel 2005). This occurs mostly with software, information, and cultural products, where firms discover that it is in their interest to cultivate an extended network of customers so that good ideas for fixing bugs or new products can flow back to the firm. Ultimately, customers should be part of a community. Businesses that encourage their user base to improve software code, spread word about a product's success, or develop fan-based cultural content can benefit immensely when it comes to the bottom line. Users help anticipate market trends, and the community network of users or fans can support each other, so they can generate a significant amount of economic value.

Yochai Benkler's argument in *The Wealth of Networks* also has immense implications for media (Benkler 2007). He argues that the social exchange of ideas creates more value than the closed ownership of ideas, such that conventional economics cannot explain why things like open source software, Wikipedia, and fan-generated culture are so successful. He finds that peer production is a growing phenomenon, because of the internet, and that it is especially threatening to big entertainment businesses that attempt to control the distribution of copyrighted material. Businesses that do not take advantage of the value that resides in social networks of peer production risk becoming economically irrelevant. And media businesses that resist this new form of cultural production by overzealously guarding intellectual property may find that their customers move on to forms of culture that are produced in the networked public sphere.

The network perspective on media economics reveals several important kinds of changes. Castells demonstrates that, over the last two decades, both the fundamentals of business have changed and the organization of the economy has changed. Many of these changes are most visible in the advanced economies, but because of network effects, they can also be seen in the urban metropolises of the global south. The networked enterprise is a peculiar organizational form that uses new technologies to integrate materials and talent for a short period of productivity on a focused product. Thus, task-based teams, more than incorporated businesses, are the important unit of analysis. From a network perspective, the key unit of the production process is not the firm, but the project.

First, a growing amount of consumer products, especially cultural products from media industries, are never really finished, they are permanently in beta form. Increasingly, software, cultural content, and even hardware are released to consumers even though their producers admit they are not finished. Second, a growing amount of economic production, especially from media industries, only gets close to being finished when you actually use the software, content, or hardware. Even if you paid for these things, your feedback as a user is what makes the product more valuable to others and brings the product design closer to completion. Third, contemporary businesses need ever more sophisticated ways of collecting and analyzing information about all aspects of their business. It is not enough to throw more money or staff into raising profits; information systems are themselves ways of creating value for a business. Moreover, a growing sector of the global economy is dedicated to information services.

Finally, the network society is not without uncertainties about the future of the media. There have been plenty of exciting new business models and innovative ways of producing and consuming culture. But many large media industries resist some aspects of the new economy, guarding copyright overzealously, lobbying against public investment in information infrastructure, discouraging technology users from being too creative. While big media conglomerates are eager to accept the benefits of participating in a network economy, they use political strategies for mitigating what they may perceive to be threats to traditional copyright law and their profit bottom line. Castells, along with prominent legal scholars like Cass Sunstein and Lawrence Lessig, have offered alternative ways of crafting intellectual property law that make more sense in a world mediated by networked and digital technologies. But even they admit that the lack of progress on these issues is mostly due to a lack of political will. And just as there is a network perspective on media economics, the network perspective on political life reveals how power operates in today's society.

3

NETWORKS OF POWER AND POLITICS

According to the network perspective, power relationships are largely defined by and through structures of communication. *Castells demonstrates multiple forms of what he calls network power—it is both the ability to project power over existing networks and the ability to construct new networks.* In *Communication Power*, Castells describes the first as a kind of "switching power" because it is the ability to direct ideas, resources, or people through to your subnetworks. He describes the second as a kind of "programming power" because it is the ability to select ideas, resources, or people and design the linkages between these things. Managing networks of social relations and media distribution is one of the most important tasks for contemporary political authority.

Castells argues, as do Arjun Appadurai and Ben Anderson, that the state has had the formidable role of keeping an economy and a culture unified through politics. The nation-state held the political authority to keep businesses and individuals united around some shared identity and sense of collective purpose. Newspapers had a crucial role in creating and sustaining new nations in Southeast Asia, as Anderson demonstrates in *Imagined Communities* (Anderson 1991). Ritualized moments of reading created the state among weak actors because newspapers and novels allowed elites to read about their country in their own language. Today, the rituals of maintaining pictures and stories on social networking applications, texting and tweeting about daily life, and keeping track of the activities of our friends and family are the ritualized ways that allow us to imagine our networks.

Both Castells and Appadurai argue that fixed and territorial relations have become much more fluid, with migrants, tourists, refugees, and labor mobility, media images of the world, trans-border communications, global capital flows, and competition from other sources of identity. For Appadurai, the political terrain can be viewed in ways that might privilege some of these elements over others, making for a fragmented and ever-shifting sense of what politics even is (Appadurai 1996). As individuals we are members of several networks at any given time. We use digital media to manage these various identities. Castells argues that media still have a role in supporting identity politics, but nation may be only one of several affinity networks to which we belong. Nationalism itself may come from very weak ties. And instead of fragmenting politics, media networks offer new opportunities for coordination and control.

Media have become the public sphere. The common spaces in which political conversations happen are in electronic networks. Face-to-face interaction is still important, but the process of political socialization primarily takes place in networked, digitized, and interactive media.

Thus, the relationship between citizens and politics, between the represented and the representative, depends essentially on what happens in this media-centered communication space. Not that the media dictate politics and policies. But it is in the media space that political battles of all kinds are fought, won and lost. (Castells 2004, 30)

The public sphere is one of the most important concepts in the social and political sciences. *The public sphere is the space—increasingly a digitally mediated space—in which people discuss cultural values, compose solutions to shared problems, and implement collective projects.*

However, there are differing ideas of what the long-term impact of digital media will be on the public sphere. For Jürgen Habermas, the public sphere is an institutional arrangement requiring shared text, room for conversation, and a place for action. Practically speaking, this means that all citizens need access to the same news content about social problems, they need to deliberate and debate about solutions, and they need a physical space to vote and administer public solutions. Ideally, all relevant voices are heard, the best arguments float to the top, and agreement is based on reason, not force or privilege (Habermas 1991).

This is one of the most widely used understandings of how a healthy public sphere should work, but it may have been crafted with evidence from a different media era. The editors of newspapers, magazines, and televised news used to perform the important task of filtering through stories, finding credible sources, and selecting items worthy of wide broadcast. In a network society, where people control and customize their own digital filters, how can there be much of a public sphere? If most citizens set up filters to manage what news topics are on their homepage, or rely on their own social networks to supply information about elections and politics, will they ever be exposed to diverse opinions? Answering these kinds of questions is a task that may fall to the next generation of media researchers. For the moment, we can answer questions about the organization of political life, and the role of media networks in structuring the production and consumption of political information.

NETWORK CAMPAIGNS

Networks are constituted by nodes and links. Networks often contain subnetworks, and an increasingly important strategy for today's tech-savvy politicians, lobbyists, and social movement leaders is to build campaigns that take advantage of the natural links of like-minded friends and family. Civic leaders hoping to gather public opinion in their favor used to create campaign strategies for large categories of people. Many different kinds of issues were bundled together and packaged for large groups of voters. Workers' rights and social welfare projects appealed to the middle class and union members. Tax relief and conservative social policies appealed to the wealthy upper classes. Political parties, at election time, assembled "platforms" that were a compilation of many different kinds of policy options.

Barack Obama's 2008 campaign for president may be one of the most high-profile examples of a networked political campaign. It deliberately supported network relations between supporters and the management team, rather than hierarchical relations. In other words, the campaign organization was as much about connections between supporters as it was between supporters and campaign management. Moreover, the campaign used digital media to maintain those relations in sophisticated ways. His campaign was described as "viral" because it relied on digital media and personal connections across communities to rapidly raise donations and call out supporters on election day. Popular social media, such as Facebook and YouTube, were sites of content produced by both average users and the campaign's affinity organizations. MyBarackObama.com had tools for allowing supporters to manage their volunteer efforts in connecting with neighbors. Data-mining efforts married computer logs from volunteers with other sources of information about income, donation history, and the likelihood of turning up to vote. These relational databases made it possible for Obama's team to narrowcast, and reproduce his political brand in nuanced ways so that most people could find some affinity with most of the policy positions he stood for.

Figure 3.1 illustrates how relations in a political campaign can be organized. At the very top of Obama's campaign organization was a fairly traditional hierarchically structured team: the candidate, senior advisors, teams of pollsters, fundraisers. Some people are at the top, and they manage the people below them. Before digital media, this hierarchical organizational form could be found all the way down through to the levels of volunteers in particular communities. Block captains, for example, would be responsible for

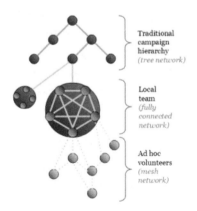

Figure 3.1: The Power of Digital Networks in Modern Political Campaigns

mobilizing their neighbors, and for collecting donations and passing those donations up the chain. But a network campaign, as exemplified by Obama's organization, cultivates a fully connected network of local managers. The campaign works to increase connections among the ad hoc network of volunteers. Doing so improves solidarity among volunteers. Sometimes YouTube, Meetup.com, Facebook, MyBarackObama.com (or a dozen other social media applications) allowed the campaign staff to build local teams and network volunteers with each other, but sometimes these tools just allowed campaign staff to build connections to community networks that already existed.

Not every modern political campaign looks like Obama's did in 2008. In other kinds of elections, voters have different views on different topics, and often find it challenging to vote because affinity with a candidate or party is often partial. We like many of the things a candidate stands for or many aspects of a party platform—but not everything. Castells demonstrates how network power allows political leaders to run different kinds of campaigns. These network campaigns reach narrow segments of the population who will be attracted to much that the candidate stands for, but also allow campaign managers to send slightly different messages to different subnetworks of supporters. This allows campaign managers to hide things they know *won't* appeal to specific subnetworks of supporters.

Another advantage of the network campaign is that it allows campaign managers to become news sources and bypass traditional news outlets. For many decades, political leaders in advanced democracies such as Australia, Canada and the U.K. had to rely on the state news broadcaster to deliver political messages to the public. The television and radio news broadcasts of the Australian Broadcasting Corporation, Canadian Broadcasting Corporation, and

British Broadcasting Corporation employed professional journalists and editors to decide what was news, interpret political events, and distribute news content to a widespread population. In the United States, the nightly television newscasters of ABC, CBS, and NBC were the brokers of political news and information.

But today, political actors use the internet to bypass the media and quickly and directly distribute their messages. Sometimes they simply seek to provoke exposure by interesting the traditional news organizations in picking up the message or image. More often, political actors develop their own media networks to help segregate the news audience from news organizations that might not echo a carefully crafted message. A growing number of U.S. citizens confess to treating the websites of the Christian Coalition, the National Rifle Association, or the Sierra Club *as* a news filtering service. Tea Party members feel that mainstream media do not do justice to conservative issues, so dedicated volunteers produce content that more closely represents group values, and this content gets passed along tight networks of Tea Party members.

In almost every recent national election—from the United States and United Kingdom to Malaysia and Russia—prominent candidates developed Facebook and Myspace profiles, collected links to their extended networks of supporters, and generated videos for YouTube. Syrian strongman Assad has a Facebook page, claiming 25,000 thousand friends.[2] They answered questions online, employed campaign bloggers, and tapped their networks for financial contributions. In the United States, President Obama's campaign developed particularly good social networking strategies. But this is not just a U.S. phenomenon: elections in Chile, Croatia, Ukraine, Sri Lanka, Greece, Colombia, and Brazil had notable network campaigns by the leading national candidates.

Network campaigns are not without risks, as Castells observes (Castells 2007). What carries forth along ties of family and friends may be jokes about politicians rather than substantive ideas from candidates for higher office. And if you are a candidate, your opponents will be well positioned to research your history and monitor your activities if they can shadow your public appearances, recording your words and gestures at different events, and track down your previous statements on key issues. Your opponents can easily publish embarrassing videos of you on YouTube. They can even compose false and scandalizing stories and images for limited distribution within subnetworks of voters to help galvanize opinion against you. And, as Stromer-Galley found, many campaign managers don't like using new media technologies because of the risk of losing control of conversations and messages (Stromer-Galley 2000).

MEDIA NETWORKS

Castells argues that Rupert Murdoch, CEO of News Corporation, is an excellent example of how one person can command network power (Arsenault and Castells, 2008a). As the CEO of an immense global media empire, Murdoch has successfully controlled the connection points, or nodes, between different business, media, and political networks. Murdoch has become a broker of political interests, has successfully leveraged public opinion, and produced sensational media content that activates particular networks of like-minded citizens. By customizing media content and diversifying media holdings, he has been able to work around technological and regulatory changes and deliver content to subnetworks of media consumers. "The NewsCorp empire spans five continents," observes Castells, "reaches approximately 75 percent of the world's population, and has approximately US$68 billion in total assets and US$28 billion in annual revenue" (Arsenault and Castells 2008b, 491).

NewsCorp controls many networks of both content production and distribution, from television, radio, film, and newspapers to books and digital media. It has a well-funded and sophisticated lobbying wing, and has donated millions to prominent political candidates around the world, some of whom (such as John McCain, Al Gore, Arnold Schwarzenegger and Tony Blair) speak at corporate retreats. Some political leaders serve on committees regulating the telecommunications industry. As Castells reveals, political leaders such as U.S. Congressman Ed Markey (D-MA) served as key backers of the 1996 Telecommunications Act, legislation that allowed NewsCorp to consolidate 20th Century Fox, TV Guide, and HarperCollins as media assets. Other political leaders with influence over telecommunications regulations are offered multi-million-dollar book publication deals. With strong personal connections to the Federal Communications Commission (FCC) in the United States, Australian media magnate Murdoch manages the only broadcast network to ever receive a waiver on U.S. foreign ownership restrictions (Arsenault and Castells 2008b).

Interestingly, what makes politicians want to participate in the NewsCorp media empire is the widespread perception that Murdoch's media properties have a significant influence over public opinion. There is some debate among political communication scholars over the degree to which particular media properties influence voter behavior. There is evidence that in the United States, however, Fox viewers are among the most ill-informed and most likely to vote Republican (Project for Excellence in Journalism 2007). This means that NewsCorp—and Murdoch himself—are important brokers between networks of politicians, networks of voters, and networks of content producers.

NewsCorp acquired MySpace.com in 2007 in a bid to enter the market for social networking applications. The appeal of MySpace.com has faded relative to Facebook (as Friendster once faded to MySpace). But as the source of print and broadcast content that is so often digitized for distribution online, NewsCorp remains one of the largest and most extensive media networks in the world. Indeed, as the source of power in the network society, it has a role in defining what the world looks like because it selects the news stories that headline across multiple news formats. What gets broadcast on the evening television news is sent out over content feeds and pushed to your mobile phone.

NewsCorp is one example of the exercise of power in media networks. In terms of revenue, News Corporation is behind The Walt Disney Company and Time Warner (respectively $36 and $25 billion in 2009). And how are Google and Microsoft not media conglomerates (respectively $24 billion and $62 billion)? On almost a daily basis many of us rely on the power of these organizations to manage our information, and both Google and Microsoft profit from the various ways they control different hardware, software, and content. As firms their investment strategies may seem very different, but on the whole they profit from providing interesting content and the infrastructure for producing, distributing, and consuming content. And they all are very good at projecting their political power when it comes to enforcing technical standards and intellectual property laws that serve their business needs.[3]

Figure 3.2 is a network map made from records of which people serve on the corporate boards of firms whose stocks are publicly traded in the United States. Each year, these corporations must file records with the Securities and Exchange Corporation, so it is possible to see how a few individuals are important ties between firms. The figure

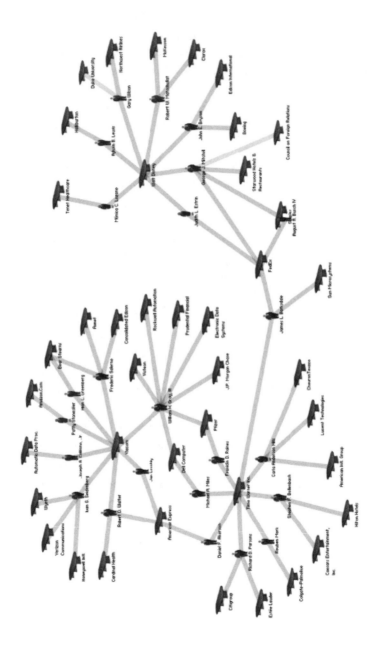

Figure 3.2: Network Relations between Media Firms, through Links between Board Members

does not reveal that businesses like Walt Disney, Viacom, or Time Warner are at the center of business networks in the United States. More accurately, it reveals that a few people connect these media empires to each other at a senior level, and that many of these board members are connected to other large corporations.

For Castells, media conglomerates are examples of good network organizations and of network power. Hollywood provides another example, both of how tightly bounded networks of cultural icons are and of how networks are constituted. The Oracle of Bacon measures how far removed—the number of weak ties—any actor has with Kevin Bacon.[4] This does not mean that Kevin Bacon is the center of the Hollywood universe. Instead it offers a simple average of the number of linkages between actors through their membership in movie casts. For example, Shia LaBeouf has a "Bacon Number" of 2: He was in the movie *Constantine* (2005) with Djimon Hounsou who was in *Beauty Shop* (2005) with Kevin Bacon. The concept behind the Bacon Number is that every Hollywood actor—or at least those listed in the Internet Movie Database (IMDB)—can be evaluated for the strength of their tie to Kevin Bacon.

There would be a few actors who have direct ties and acted in the same movie with Kevin Bacon. There would be many more with only weak ties. Moreover, some actors would be more central to the network than others. Even though Dennis Hopper passed away in 2010, he is the "best center" of the Hollywood universe because every actor is on average 2.7 steps away from him. Hopper is so central because he had a long career, acted in good movies and bad, and starred in movies of many genres with big casts. These kinds of network ties can be found among journalists, dot-com employees, and other media industries. Network ties are not unique within media industries, but they are all the more apparent because of the importance of media in our public sphere and the fact that so much media work involves temporary, networked teams.[5]

Studying media networks can mean looking at the ways in which media conglomerates hold particular forms of power, which they maintain by being so central to the production and distribution of culture. It can also mean observing how networks are structured, by using relational databases such as the IMDB. A researcher could study cultural production in Hollywood by many methods, but the network perspective reveals particular things about power and structure in the relationships between actors.

THE POLITICS OF CODE AND CULTURAL PRODUCTION

There are several ways of challenging the media power held by people such as Murdoch. By definition, media networks can serve a few people who broker many relationships. So in network societies two forms of resistance to power can reside in individuals: the power to redistribute content to their own networks of family and friends; and the power to create their own content, which they can choose to distribute without using the battery of legal protections in traditional copyright law.

One of Castells' mentors, Nicos Poulantzas, wrote that social movements "exhibit a characteristic anti-statism and express themselves in the mushrooming of self-management centres [sic] and networks of direct intervention by the mass in the decisions which affect them" (Poulantzas and Camiller 2001, 246). In an important way, Castells continues to use this notion of network power in the same way his teacher used it. Digital media works because of code that greatly decentralizes the means of cultural production, and allows self-forming networks to share content and flout state laws about content rights. For Castells, digital media is a particularly good information infrastructure for supporting those social movements that seek more influence in political processes.

According to the Pew Internet and American Life Project, 69 percent of internet users in the United States—36 million U.S. citizens—had downloaded music or video content using the internet by 2005. About half this population use peer-to-peer networks or paid online services to share their files, and the proportion of people doing this has certainly increased since the study was done (Pew Internet and American Life Project 2005). Many of the people sharing content through peer-to-peer networks are among the youngest of internet users. They feel that the industry response of suing its customers revealed a lack of understanding of the network society and an inability to transition to new business models.

But the political activity of redistributing content can take many forms. In Italy, pirate radio stations and street television such as Tele Orfeo are fed audio and video content through peer-to-peer networks. In his role as the prime minister of Italy, Silvio Berlusconi so successfully manages both his privately held media assets and the public broadcasters that the most genuinely independent sources of political opposition are found online. Paris has Zalea TV, Barcelona has Okepum les Ones, Buenos Aires has TV Piquetera, and Seattle has its Seattle Wireless Community. Such projects do not necessarily violate copyright law, but may actively produce content under rival regimes of intellectual property. Several scholars, including Castells and Gillespie, have demonstrated the peculiar, inconsistent, and contradictory ways that media conglomerates use politicians to craft laws that protect intellectual property (Gillespie 2009). So along with redistributing content to networks of family and friends, individuals have the power to generate content and distribute it without buying into the traditional codes of intellectual property.

In *Convergence Culture*, Henry Jenkins explores the new, varied ways in which culture is produced over digital networks. Jenkins uses more creative terms to describe what Castells sees as a very political process. What is unique to contemporary cultural production, according to Jenkins, is that both savvy media artists and average consumers learn how culture works by breaking it down into its most basic building blocks, and then rebuilding it in creative ways (Jenkins 2006). This is what allows images, ideas, and narratives to flow across multiple media channels. With basic consumer electronics, digital content can easily be archived, annotated, appropriated, and recirculated. While this is certainly a creative process, doing these things becomes a political act when major media interests work hard to over-extend their copyright claims.

Lessig plumbs the relationship between software code and law more deeply. He shows that even though history is replete with examples of how artistic masters refashion old works into new ones, today's cultural industries have successfully used copyright law to protect their intellectual property and punish the artists of derivative works (Lessig 2004). This means that producing free culture, or supporting creative commons licenses, are ways of resisting the authority of network power.[6]

There are certainly other ways of opposing the network power of elite corporate, political, and cultural interests. The anti-globalization movement is better able to attract new members from around the world, and better able to mobilize its sympathizers for everything from economic boycott to street-level protest. The Indymedia movement makes use of cheap consumer electronics to document social injustice, often in real time. Being an activist in the network society requires a distinct set of skills, tools, and tactics, and Castells has demonstrated that social movements from Korea, the Philippines, Thailand, and Nepal to Ecuador, the Ukraine, or France are either new or newly successful for their sophisticated use of information technologies (Castells 2010).

He goes so far as to argue that these newly empowered network activists have taken away top jobs from political leaders. A spontaneous mobilization of Spanish youth in March 2004, armed with mobile phones, brought down Prime Minister Aznar for his devious attempts to manipulate public opinion about the Madrid massacre. This is not a technological effect, Castells points out, "but the ability of a network technology to distribute horizontally messages that resonate with the public consciousness in ways that are trustworthy" (Castells 2007, 251). Yet this is also a point in which Castells receives some criticism. After all, political elites often seem more adept at using technologies than grassroots activists, and political processes are so complex that it can be difficult to really identify a prominent political leader who won office *because* of his or her digital media strategy.

PRIVACY AND DATA MINING

Like Lawrence Lessig, Castells argues that the political power used to reside in the state's threat of physical violence but now resides in its authority over the terms and conditions of communication. Lessig may have the more evolved argument here, since he convincingly demonstrates the range of ways in which the technical codes of consumer electronics and public information infrastructure become ways of governing and surveilling citizens (Lessig 2006). *Privacy is the power to control what other people know about you, and other people can use digital media to learn about you either by monitoring your activities or by searching for information about you.* Castells and Lessig share the perspective that the real world is not just what happens offline. Non-users of the internet are vulnerable to privacy violations because digital information about them is held by other people and organizations that are online.

There are many factors that went into the electoral defeat of Spanish Prime Minister Aznar in 2004, as there are many reasons Obama won the U.S. presidential election in 2008. It would be difficult to say that internet or mobile phone strategy caused these political outcomes, and there would surely be more prominent and proximate causes for these outcomes. Whereas Castells argues that it is increasingly difficult for governments to hide or manipulate information because such manipulations are immediately picked up by networks of citizen activists, yet there are also new ways for governments to collect vast amounts of information about people, and the fact that we have caught some impressive government manipulations does not indicate a decline in elite manipulation. Probably the worst of these manipulations involved the U.S. Administration's poor intelligence and active maneuvers toward war in Iraq under President Bush.

But in the freshly securitized U.S., network technologies play a key role in monitoring the attitudes and behaviors of U.S. citizens. Moreover, the commercial data-mining industry is ever more sophisticated, building complex relational databases that allow powerful inferences about attitudes and behaviors from vast databases of credit card records, medical histories, and tax records. This means that the ability of corporate and government surveillance to violate what most people consider to be privacy norms is as high as ever.

THE NETWORK PERSPECTIVE ON
POLITICAL LIFE

The network perspective on political life helps us explain the prominence of many contemporary political actors such as Murdoch, Obama, and Berlusconi. But it also helps us interpret what we see at election time in many countries. Prominent political actors reveal who their backers are, and winning politicians often have an impressive network of corporate and individual donors. High-profile political leaders who do not win the post they are running for retire to well-paid positions on corporate boards of multinational firms.[7]

U.S. President Obama led an innovative campaign strategy for the White House in 2008. Obama got his supporters to post political content online, engage their social networks in political conversations, share multimedia content, subscribe to campaign updates and news feeds, donate funds, and volunteer online. Obama's volunteers did these things much more than McCain's volunteers (Pew Internet and American Life Project 2008).

Berlusconi, the long-serving prime minister of Italy, has also proven himself a master of network power: he effectively controls 90 percent of national television broadcasting through either personal ownership or political administration; has changed the statute of limitations to prevent charges of political and legal manipulation from being filed; and has aggressively pursued journalists who research and publicize his dealings. Whereas political battles in Italy used to involve political parties and protest in public squares, today political contestation is most centrally found in the media. And the confluence of media power is easy to observe in other advanced democracies, such as Canada, Australia, and the United Kingdom. For those of us interested in political communication, studying contemporary forms of activism has been particularly difficult because many of the things that are easy to observe as formal outcomes—such as voter turn-out or affiliation with a political party—are at all-time lows. People may have less trust in the government or established political actors, but they still have opinions and interest in civic life. The network perspective on political life must take into account that the things that count as politics may have more to do with lifestyle choices and consumer activism, and may not look like formal political behavior.

For example, in Castells' study of his own Catalan community, he found that while only 1 percent of those surveyed were involved in the activities of political parties, over 50 percent did not trust parties or governments, over 33 percent were engaged in alternative associations and movements of various kinds, and over 70 percent believed they could "influence the world" through their own social mobilization (Castells et al. 2003). Moreover, he found a distinct causal sequencing involving the adoption of new technologies. Young Catalans with autonomous personal, professional, political, or communicative projects are more likely to actively use the internet. The more they use the internet, the more autonomous they become with regard to political and media institutions.

4

CULTURAL INDUSTRIES IN A
DIGITAL CENTURY

Culture is a difficult thing to define. It includes strange
social practices, it resides in peculiar artifacts, and it includes
the media that are purposely built to communicate those
practices. For Castells, the network perspective allows for
several insights into cultural production. "Because culture
is mediated and enacted through communication, cultures
themselves—that is, our historically produced systems of
beliefs and codes—become fundamentally transformed, and
will be more so over time, by the new technology system"
(Castells 1996, 357). Culture can include norms and symbols, but material culture can have a very concrete form in
food, painting, and digital media.

What is culture? *From a network perspective, culture is the
relations of production, consumption, power, and experience—
along with the information infrastructure that supports these
relations.* Castells is one of a number of thinkers who actually
defines culture in terms of technology, and defines technology in terms of culture. His working definition of culture

is significantly shaped by the notion of "material culture" expressed by Claude Fischer. In Fischer's book, *America Calling*, material culture refers to the instruments with which and the conditions within which we live our lives (Fischer 1994). For Fischer, the telephone was the functional and symbolic center of a social transformation that occurred in the early part of the twentieth century—a communication tool that transformed the way lives were lived. If we accept, as Castells does, that material culture has a role in social change and exemplifies social change, then digital media may be the functional and symbolic center of social transformation today.

How do new media technologies transform culture? Digital media overcome the lag of time and space that used to slow down cultural production and consumption, and keep these things locally compartmentalized. Liberating social interaction from the constraints of time and the burden of geography creates a "space of flows" where we find a lot of cultural production and consumption in network societies. The space of flows concept is discussed in Chapter 5, "The Space of Flows and Timeless Time," pp. 78–81. In the previous chapters the death of distance and synchronicity of communication had clear consequences for the way we run businesses and the way we do politics. The space of flows is also noticeably unique when it comes to cultural production and consumption.[8] Perhaps the most concrete transformation has been in the organization of cultural industries.

TRANSFORMING CULTURAL INDUSTRIES

Many cultural industries, such as fashion, film, and video games, have had to radically reorganize in response to the new information and communication technologies. The transformation of the way in which cultural content, such as television and music, is produced and distributed is peculiar. On the one hand, argues Castells, cultural industries are increasingly concentrated in media conglomerates such as NewsCorp, Bertelsmann, and Time Warner. A few firms own a wide range of media assets that produce and distribute content across multiple broadcast and print formats. On the other hand, cultural industries produce multi-format content that greatly complicates the comparability of cultural products.

By 2008 the top-grossing video games were generating better revenues than many Hollywood films. The first-day revenue record for any kind of entertainment product goes to the video game *Halo 3*, which earned US$170 million in 2007. That same year, *Spiderman 3* earned US$59 million on its opening day. Yet adding in international sales and looking at the long term, *Spiderman 3* has grossed US$890 million and *Halo 3* US$389 million. A more recent film, *Avatar*, has grossed US$2.7 billion. As a cultural product, *Avatar* made extensive use of digitization techniques developed in the video game industry and advanced the digital arts in ways that will have an immense impact on other cultural industries. With films that generate narratives for video games, and video game production tools that improve the special effects in films, does it make sense to distinguish contemporary cultural products on the basis of the form in which a consumer experiences a story?

Still, the success of these businesses lies in their ability to segment media markets and provide particular kinds of cultural content to distinct communities. So while the cultural industries have become oligopolistic, they must customize the delivery of their content and be vertically integrated in the sense of employing artists to create, sales staff to sell, and infrastructure to deliver. Branded content is especially important, as Disney or Pixar will attest, because such content can be easily ported from platform to platform and remain recognizable to consumers. Batman, after all, can generate revenue for the makers of toys, movies, video games, cartoons, and comic books. When confronted about the rapid drop in *Playboy*'s circulation (a drop from 7 million in the 1970s to 1.5 million in 2010), Hugh Hefner responded that "to begin with, it was the magazine that carried the brand; now the brand carries the magazine" (Solomon 2010).

Because digital media allow content across multiple platforms, it makes sense for the big players in cultural industries to collaborate through partnerships and investments. Content owners want to see their material reach people over mobile phones and through movie theaters; infrastructure owners want to profit by controlling as many distribution channels as possible. The result, as Castells and numerous other media scholars point out, is industry consolidation and technology convergence.

In Figure 4.1, Arsenault and Castells demonstrate some of the important relations between media firms (Arsenault and Castells 2008a). Since this was published in 2008, some of these relationships have dissolved and others have been deepened. And while this figure reveals the strong linkages of partnerships and cross-investments, it does not reveal many of the temporary and short-term relationships that form with the ebb and flow of cultural production. We may think of *Iron Man 2*, for example, primarily as a film. But many of these organizations would be temporarily involved in a web of relations to promote the film online, distribute film trailers through game consoles, advertise on search engines, produce video games, and coordinate an international distribution to however many theaters on a single release date.

Perhaps one of the great ironies in modern cultural industries is that the pressure to narrowly distribute

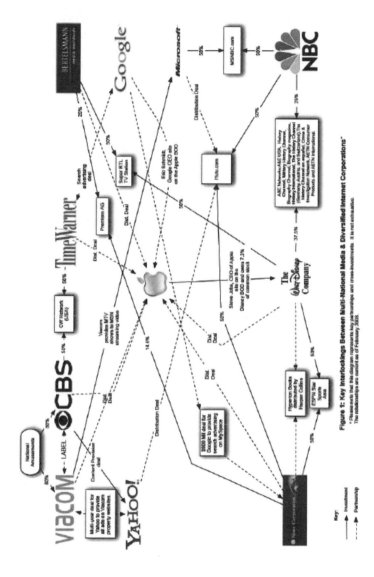

Figure 4.1: *Network Relations between Media Firms, through Links of Ownership and Content Distribution*

content to segmented markets is best relieved through corporate consolidation. In other words, the large, networked distribution channels are really good for sending small groups of consumers particular content on particular media platforms.

Despite these impressive levels of coordination, some cultural industries seem on the edge of failure. News agencies are struggling to find ways to package journalism and profit, while cultural memes from YouTube make their way into video games, movies, and commercials.[9] *Memes are contagious ideas that compete with each other for attention and longevity. Just as genes are the basic building blocks of life, memes are the smallest components of culture.* Content aggregators, mirroring sites, and peer-to-peer sharing networks blur the distinctions between producers and consumers of cultural value. This chapter contrasts the traditional, hierarchical means of cultural production before the internet with how cultural production works now. But to understand the impact of digital media on culture, we must first understand the uniqueness of digital media culture. The global, simultaneous viewing of a modern Hollywood blockbuster film by thousands of people on thousands of screens is a good example of how the space of cultural flows is coordinated in astounding ways through digital media.

CULTURES OF DIGITAL MEDIA

Castells is most eager to explain the big picture: structural changes in the way we produce and consume culture. These structures of production and consumption support a wide range of particular and peculiar cultural content. Such content does not have to have originated in a network society. For example, even though Spiderman comics were produced and distributed long before the internet, today's kids get

Spiderman content in varied forms and it is produced by a very different kind of cultural industry. The industry that entertained adults with the edgy and irreverent *Flintstones* is organized differently from the one that entertains adults with the edgy and irreverent *Family Guy*. But just as important as these large-scale changes in cultural industries are the four particular cultures that are distinct to information societies.

> The culture of the Internet is a culture made up of a technocratic belief in the progress of humans through technology, enacted by communities of hackers thriving on free and open technological creativity, embedded in virtual networks aimed at reinventing society, and materialized by money-driven entrepreneurs into the workings of the new economy. (Castells 2001, 61)

The first special culture of information societies is the techno-meritocratic culture that most internet pioneers shared. Many of the big names who designed the hardware and software of digital media shared norms similar to those held in academe. Computer scientists—like most scientists—value the pursuit of new knowledge and cherish their role in advancing collective projects. The highest rewards are not monetary, but appreciation from the community of peers. While information infrastructure was bought and paid for by military money, many of the individuals who designed the information infrastructure were not military men. They worshiped clean code, believed in sharing, and participated in collective projects.

This culture of techno-meritocracy still exists today. Wikipedia represents the collective knowledge and writing craft of thousands of volunteers. These volunteers work hard to improve the content of Wikipedia. The open source movement continues to generate technical standards and provide software free of the encumbrances of digital rights management. These coders improve Apache software for servers, Ubuntu software for computers, and OpenOffice applications for individual users.

The second special culture of information societies is that of hackers. Just as internet pioneers valued building information technology as a creative challenge, hackers enjoy the craft of disassembling and reassembling information technologies. They look for unexplored applications and design weaknesses. They have been maligned by major news media and big corporations, but the "hacker ethic" does not condone criminal activity. Instead, hackers are more appropriately seen as tinkerers and hobbyists. When you buy a car, aren't you allowed to personalize it, explore its workings, and do things to improve its performance? When you buy a computer, shouldn't you be allowed to personalize it, explore its workings, and do things to improve its performance? If a Linksys router comes with firmware that does not make full use of the hardware, hackers will help find ways to flash the memory with software that lets the consumer get more out of the equipment they paid for.

Hackers like to be independent of the big technology corporations, and they resist attempts to criminalize their work or constrain them by unfair "user agreements" that some technologies now come with. Like the techno-meritocratic internet pioneers, hackers champion open software and sometimes contribute to improving product design by showing firms security holes. They certainly push the boundaries of user agreements and sometimes the law. If you maintain a Wi-Fi access point and decide to make it publicly accessible, do you have the right to monitor the packets of traffic that travel over your equipment? Hacker culture believes in the freedom of information and deplores the concentration of media power.

Castells believes that virtual communities are a third culture unique to the information society. *Virtual communities are distributed networks of individuals who share a common interest, provide mutual support, and have particular, collectively agreed sets of norms, rules, and patterns of interaction.* Indeed, by definition virtual cultures are those groups whose exclusive means of socialization are online. Since the very beginning of the internet, communities have formed around games, art, entertainment, politics, and hobbies. Massively multiplayer online games draw in millions of users to join guilds, live in alternative worlds, and interact in digital media. Sometimes such communities have offline interactions, but political chat rooms and dating forums provide a strong virtual community. As Castells points out, just because such communities are virtual does not mean they are unreal.

One of the pioneers of research on digital culture is Howard Rheingold, whose books *The Virtual Community* and *Smart Mobs* make the convincing argument that digital media support wonderfully rich forms of social interaction (Rheingold 2000; 2002). The first book is an important, almost ethnographic, exploration of how community norms developed in one of the first internet forums. The second extends the argument that such online communities are important and unique cultures to say that they have immense potential for collective action. Together, these two works have convinced many people, including Castells, that digital media support and extend community in interesting ways.

While Wikipedia is a good example of a techno-meritocratic community, it is also a good example of a virtual community. While many people supply content for Wikipedia, it is a smaller subset of community members who do the important work of maintaining quality control. Wikipedians monitor the entries, and watch out for spam or political interference from corporations and governments. They ensure that the professors listed there are publicly important. Other virtual communities form around games or products. *World of Warcraft*, a massively multiplayer online game, has 12 million subscribers. Coffee aficionados review the latest home espresso-making equipment on YouTube. And people join virtual communities when they hit major transitions in their life course or at difficult times in their lives. Victims of crime or addiction commune with others who have suffered. Young men and women discuss the meaning of love in cultures where marriages are arranged. With these common interests and digital networks, people often find themselves giving and receiving social support in ways not directly related to the mission of the group, and this is what makes virtual communities especially vibrant.

The fourth culture that is unique to information societies is that of the digital entrepreneur. These individuals transformed business practices by commercializing the internet. The culture of entrepreneurship turned what was once an infrastructure connecting universities and military installations into media we have at home, work, and in our pockets. Cults of personality evolve around the individuals who made and lost fortunes giving us digital media, and companies often promote the image of their rogue, visionary founders.

The Microsoft story is not told without Bill Gates and the Apple story is not told without Steve Jobs. Even after the dot-com boom and bust that ended many entrepreneurial projects, Mark Zuckerberg is an important part of Facebook's corporate mythology and Sergey Brinis an important part of Google's corporate mythology. This entrepreneurial culture sometimes overlaps with the other three, sometimes it comes into conflict with the other three. Many of these inspiring leaders developed their technologies in university settings, dabbled as hackers, and participated in virtual communities of like-minded computer scientists. But eager to commercialize technologies, they believe that patents and proprietary ideas do more to make technology accessible. The way to build a network society is through firms that can profit by producing new commercial electronics, the entrepreneurs believe.

These four cultures—techno-elites, hackers, virtual communitarians, and digital entrepreneurs—both built the information society and are of the internet. But Castells does not just argue that there are cultures unique to digital media. Ultimately, he argues that digital media have transformed whole cultural industries and even the way we compose our identity.

SOCIAL NETWORKING AND CULTURAL PRODUCTION

What Castells teaches us is that digital media enhance our ability to manage our own identity, but as a consequence we do so within the context of our social networks. So while we can choose to submit videos to YouTube, maintain a blog, or personalize an online profile, all of that kind of cultural production is for our social network. Many of the technologies we use and digital artifacts we create are purpose-built for our networks of friends, family, and work colleagues. Culture, as Castells uses the term, is not just norms, values, and patterns of behavior. It has a substantial form in information technology.

Digital media support different sizes and kinds of networks. The network society is constituted by our own personal relations with family, friends, and work colleagues. It is also constituted by ties between places that are not geographically near each other. Communicating between London and New York took weeks by ship and days by post.

With a broadband connection, it takes fractions of seconds to send an email or upload a file to the internet. For social purposes, this is a measure of time that is so small as to be pretty much instantaneous. So the network society is also made up of global cities. Not all of Toronto, Buenos Aires, or Madrid is a global city. Most parts of these cities are very locally grounded. But some segments of these cities are so closely linked to other spaces around the world that physically proximate neighborhoods are socially distant. Gentrified Bloor West in Toronto may have more in common with La Ricoletta in Buenos Aires or Double Bay in Sydney than it has with some of the tougher neighborhoods in Toronto.

Cultural products such as video games, music, and movies increasingly translate across media. Productions we still call "television programs" are streamed to computers and mobile phones, broadcast television or cable, and video game consoles. What is the "show" *30 Rock*? For the moment, there are few labels for cultural content produced by a broadcast network (such as NBC) that is distributed over multiple platforms (such as an Xbox) or viewed while riding a bus (on a mobile phone). We may be uncertain about whether to call *30 Rock* a television show. But it is safe to say that digital media make the creation, distribution and consumption of this kind of cultural content possible.

Yet the audience is also different. Mass media made sense, as a term, because large numbers of people watched the same television programs, read the same newspapers, and went to the same movies. From the point of view of cultural industries, audiences were uniform and unindividuated and could be reached through a couple of distinct media. Newspapers and magazines contained textual content, radio transmitted audio content, and television and film had their own distinct properties. Today, text appears in print and digital form, video appears on televisions, computer screens, and mobile phones, and movies take the form of film reels, DVDs, and files on peer-to-peer sharing networks.

Cultural products come with various forms of what many scholars, including Castells, call hypertext. *This is meta-information that allows for social tagging and creating linking patterns to other digital artifacts, and it is a way of building small communities around cultural products.* What fashion designers would not want young women to promote their goods through "haul videos" on YouTube? When audiences interact with the actors of a show such as *Firefly*, they get drawn into the community to the point of co-producing the show by participating in story creation and promoting the show over their own networks.[10] Castells argues that most cultural expressions are enclosed in a symbolic hypertext that allows producers to distribute to narrow audiences over diverse technologies. In fact, transmitting cultural products through social networks, rather than mass-media advertising, has helped create new forms of cultural identity.

MEDIATED AND MULTIPLE IDENTITIES

Before the network society, major identity categories (in the United States and Europe) included race, gender, religion, class, and nation. Of course, people have always had multiple identities. But when states collected census data they only asked about these categories; marketing agencies advertised goods and cultural industries created content based on their evaluation of these categories; politicians played to these categories; social scientists collected data on these categories.

Digital media allow for much more individual control in the production and consumption of culture. In important ways, we get to set up our own cultural filters through software settings. And we can choose to develop cultural products for even the smallest affinity communities. Even when Amazon.com recommends books for us or Netflix.com recommends movies for us, the cultural feed is based on knowledge of other content we have enjoyed more than on demographic assumptions.

Consumption identities—what we might more simply call fandom—have existed as long as cultural goods have been produced. *Star Trek* fans were nutty long before they had internet access. Yet is only with digital media that fans have been able to produce amateur videos completing the USS Enterprise's five-year mission.[11] In the network society, consumption identities now involve roles in co-production: contributing reviews, promoting merchandise to friends and family, submitting ideas to improve the product or advance the story line. Savvy firms and politicians also try to build digital community around their products or candidacy, because linking up your devoted supporters translates into revenues or votes. From the point of view of individuals, brand communities are increasingly important sources of identity, and sometimes we even spend more time on our consumption identity than we do on other forms of identity.

We have not had to give up our major identity categories. But we can take more direct control of how important they are for our daily lives. Many of us feel strong affiliations for our nation, but if we are Quebequois, Catalan, or Welsh, we can use new media to actively participate in the production and consumption of these identities. In a world in which cultural industries must produce cultural content for broadcast, managers do their market analysis and support television programs and films that will interest a wide range of consumers based on broad cultural categories. In a network society, where cultural industries can narrowcast content—recall the notion of the "long tail" in Chapter 2—

managers can use networks to create content that is relevant to people who value other sources of cultural identity.

This also means that we can use digital media to keep our multiple identities active. Marrying a U.S. citizen and living in the United States can make a Canadian feel more Canadian. Using digital media to maintain symbolic ties, to commiserate with the Canadian diaspora, and get news from home makes it all bearable. Before digital media, culture was much more physically sited. Music and food were regionally specific, and a novelty when found in other places. These things were transported to other regions only as people migrated or as the occasional explorer traveled across continents. Today, we easily find new musics and exotic recipes online. As Castells points out, some urban areas become glocal in that cultures which developed far apart become physically proximate in the global city. They become socially proximate online.

THE NETWORK PERSPECTIVE ON CULTURAL LIFE

Digital media have an important role in destabilizing social structure. According to Castells, they have an especially prominent role in destabilizing the mass-media structures of cultural production and consumption. The cultural institutions that formed around mass media assumed central, physically grounded nodes of production: television studios, radio stations, Hollywood lots. Cultural consumers were also physically sited in living rooms, movie theaters, and music halls. How many of these assumptions are still safe? Some television shows like *Sanctuary* are shot in Vancouver, where the city's alleyways are meant to look like New York City or green screens recreate Mumbai. Reality television shows may not even be shot in the studio. The producers of studio-based or reality-based shows cannot guarantee that their audience is in the living room, watching at peak times between 5:00 and 9:00 pm. Instead video content is streamed online, distributed to mobile phones, cropped by fans, and embedded in hypertext.

The network perspective on cultural life foregrounds two important features of how we produce, distribute, and consume all forms of content. Digital media create a space of cultural flows that makes territorially distant places feel nearby. Cultural value and cultural capital come through connection to the network. Without access to information technologies, would we discover as many new artists? Without digital media, would we pass along as many jokes and personal anecdotes to friends and family? Would innovative video projects and fashion designs have the same international distribution channels without the internet? What we know of other cultures very much depends on their connection to a network.

First, cultural industries have used new media technologies to transform the way they work and how they produce culture. Second, as individuals we use digital media to compose our own cultural identities and affiliations in creative new ways. Our identities have always been plural, but now we have the digital media to satisfy our interests. Our identities have always been multiple, but now we have the digital media to reinforce the cultural affiliations that we value, not just the ones that institutions of nation or religion impose upon us. Moreover, consumption cultures thrive over network media, drawing the audiences and consumers for cultural products into the creative processes.

5

MOBILE AND SOCIAL MEDIA

If digital media have encouraged changes in the way economic, political, and cultural life is organized, has there been an impact on the way we organize our own lives? If we are better able to build and manage our own social networks, and mobile technologies allow us to do so from wherever we connect to a communication network, can we leverage the power of networks the way economic, political, and cultural elites do? The answer to these questions, in part, can come by looking at Castells' work on mobility and social media. "Even accounting for the differential diffusion in developing countries and poor regions," Castells points out, "a very high proportion of the population of the planet has access to mobile communication, sometimes in areas where there is no electricity but there is some form of coverage and mobile chargers of mobile batteries in the form of merchant bicycles" (Castells 2007, 246).

It used to make sense to distinguish between the real world and the virtual world, or between face-to-face and online interaction. Digital media, mobile phones, and social networking applications have changed all that. Over the last decade, we have come to learn that the "real world" is not what happens offline. Indeed, our social worlds include many kinds of interaction with interesting people and diverse forms of content. And in our personal lives many of us intuit some qualitative differences between the behaviors and attitudes of our friends and family members who have grown up in different media environments. Parents have grown up in substantively different media environments from those in which their children are living (see Figure 5.1). Even older siblings have distinct technology habits compared to their younger brothers and sisters.

Chapter 4 began with the hypothesis that digital media might be the functional and symbolic center of recent social transformations. There are many different kinds of software and hardware that play a part in this transformation.

Figure 5.1: Two Babies Play with Baby Apps on the Latest iPhone

But, the most globally pervasive, socially ubiquitous, digital networking device is the mobile phone.

Castells argues that digital media encourage mass self-communication. *This is the process by which individuals generate their own content, decide who can access the content, and directly disseminate the content to recipients who themselves can self-select whether or not to receive the content.*

> The emergence of mass self-communication offers an extraordinary medium for social movements and rebellious individuals to build their autonomy and confront the institutions of society in their own terms and around their own projects. Naturally, social movements are not originated by technology, they use technology. But technology is not simply a tool, it is a medium, it is a social construction with its own implications. (Castells 2007, 249)

Still, digital networks *are* social networks in that they are the primary conduit for the important stuff of social relationships: social capital and cultural capital.

If social capital is who you know, cultural capital is what you know. In *Bowling Alone*, Robert Putnam develops the definition of social capital that many scholars, including Castells, adopt. Social capital refers to the norms of trust and reciprocity that help overcome collective action problems, and social capital resides in your network of family and friends. In other words, you as an individual may not have social capital, but there is social capital in your network (Putnam 2001). In *Distinction*, Pierre Bourdieu develops the definition of cultural capital that many scholars, including Castells, adopt. Cultural capital refers to the habits, experiences, comportment, and education that parents pass to children and schools pass to students. You as an individual have cultural capital, and it is through cultural capital that social institutions reproduce themselves. Particular forms of knowledge and skill make you a valuable addition to a network, because these things allow you to contribute more and get more from membership in the network (Bourdieu 1987).

As scholars, Putnam probably makes more use of the network perspective than Bourdieu, but Castells makes use of the notion of both social and cultural capital to describe what it is that moves along digital networks. Digital media are a set of tools for maintaining and spending our social capital, and a way of obtaining new forms of cultural capital. Sophistication with digital media tools is a source of cultural capital because in forming new friendships, developing professional networks, and flirting, we must be able to send email, text messages, and maintain an online identity. Broadcast media such as television, radio, and newspapers do not so easily allow people to manage the social capital in their own networks. And these traditional media may broadcast cultural capital, but do not allow people to distribute their own cultural capital or collect cultural capital on their own terms.

For Castells, this is what is most important, and more social, about digital media. These technologies allow people to generate their own content, manage who can access the content, disseminate the content directly, and allow recipients the power to filter what they receive. The power of mass self-communication may be what makes digital media so attractive to us. Today, it is through digital media that we collect and spend our social and cultural capital. Indeed, informational literacy and comfort with the fast pace of change in digital media have become a form of cultural capital.

Perhaps the best example of all of these features is the mobile phone. The mobile phone represents the convergence of several technologies: they come with built-in cameras, alarm clocks, calendars, games, music players, FM radios, and keyboards; they send and receive voice, text, and video. They are among the most ubiquitous devices on the planet, with well over 1.5 billion mobile phones (certainly more than the number of fixed landlines). So the most social of media is also the most mobile of media.

Why have mobile and social media become such an important part of our daily lives? Many technologies that support mobility and social networking are easily available as consumer electronics. Market competition keeps prices low and relates the demand for mobility and social networking to the supply of innovative new communication tools. Indeed, mobile technologies have introduced new patterns of sociability. Staying connected and updating your network about your activities are now social norms in many families and communities, even though not everyone does these things at the same rate. And, many of us desire individual autonomy in our media, preferring to stream our favorite movies and television shows by filtering out ads.

NETWORKED AND MOBILE

When you build a new building, construction often proceeds in phases. So it may be useful to distinguish between several phases of the construction of a network society. At first, the internet became an important new information infrastructure because it connected computers over great distances. The collection of technologies that became the internet included undersea trunk cables, single servers, large server farms, and the software protocols that allowed different kinds of computers to share information. But the devices that most people used to connect to the internet were large computers fixed in place, hardwired to both an internet connection and a power supply.

The next stage in the construction of a network society came when a growing number of people started using their mobile phones to coordinate their personal networks of family and friends—and they liked doing this while mobile. All in all, mobile phones diffused more rapidly than computers, partly because they were less expensive and partly because they were comparatively simple technologies. Mobile phones became a way of connecting to the internet, and today they are certainly used for much more than phone calls.

With the infrastructure of server nodes and internet connections (wired and wireless) well in place, the final stage in the construction of a network society came with the development of social network applications. Software that allows users to produce content, manage content dissemination, and filter incoming content, actually allowed the mass self-communication that Castells so eloquently describes. So the transition to a network society is not just marked by the arrival of the internet. The culture of mobility and the ability to manage personal networks in sophisticated ways also distinguishes a network society. There have always been social networks. But an extensive infrastructure for networked communications, mobile technologies for accessing the network infrastructure, and software for managing social relations are important and new phenomena.

Yet it is not just that people are mobile in the network society. Today, it is reasonable to assume that young workers will rely on their weak ties to find jobs, and that these weak ties may give them access to employment opportunities in cities they have never been to. It is reasonable to assume that the mobile phone in your hand is itself a manifestation of network relations: petrochemicals from Western Australia, supplying plastics factories in China, and chip manufacturers in Taiwan; assembly in Korea and packaging in Mexico;

distribution networks that bring the finished product to you on the basis of some recommendation from someone in your social network. In addition to personal and product mobility, information is distinctly mobile in the network society. The network society is a system of circulating ideas about what modernity can and should be: perhaps the greatest casualty of this circulation is our sense of space and time.

THE SPACE OF FLOWS AND TIMELESS TIME

In important ways, global cities such as London, Toronto, and New York have more in common with each other than they do with regional capitals in their respective countries. This urban culture is a result of distinct network phenomena. One of the most important of Castells' ideas, an idea that has had an impact across the social sciences and humanities, concerns what he calls the "space of flows" and "timeless time." Both notions were introduced in his three-volume set on *The Information Age*, a set of books written before the widespread diffusion of mobile technologies and social networking applications. But a good test of the strength of the idea is its continued relevance even when things change. The concept of the space of flows may be even more relevant now that mobility and social networking applications are so important in how we conduct our daily affairs. And timeless time will seem a very intuitive notion to people who have grown up in the network society.

It has been one of Castells' most poignant observations that many digital technologies upset both our personal sense of how time passes and our sense of social distance. In a way, the new media technologies annihilate time because our way of imagining and measuring time during communications is too slow in the digital age. Letters take days to cross the country, flights across oceans take hours, phone calls happen in real time. We know something of the process of these kinds of communication: the procedure for writing letters and the person who delivers the mail; the routes and routines of traveling by air; the context in which someone answers a landline telephone and the manners by which we have phone conversations. They are modes of communication that link people at great distances, but social interaction is comparatively slow through their use. *A space of flows is the location through which media infrastructure allows for social life from different locations to proceed as if the locations are actually present and proximate. In Castells' words, it is "social simultaneity without territorial contiguity."*

But digital technologies work in ways we don't always understand and certainly have difficulty visualizing. Most of us don't fully understand hypertext, the translation to binary digits, the movement of electrons, and the infrastructure that makes use of the public spectrum that are parts of the digital communication process. When we call someone on the mobile phone we may know little of the social context—much less the geographic location—in which the phone is answered. Email and online chat are sometimes synchronous, sometimes asynchronous, forms of communication. The timestamps that are embedded in email are not always socially accurate. The speed at which messages, content, and capital spread over digital networks is so fast that, compared to the pace of human conversation, email communication is instant.

Instead of saying that digital media annihilate time, it may be more accurate to say that the passing of communication time is eliminated to the point of not being socially relevant. The time to produce and consume content may have meaning; the time to distribute content not so. In this way, the space of flows is a concept meant to capture the material arrangements for simultaneous social interaction without territorial contiguity. Social interaction used to be territorially based and territorially bounded; now it resides in the flood of information over digital networks.[12]

So the important feature of this kind of space is that people, resources, and relationships course through it. In doing so, they disrupt our traditional sense of time and temporality. Anthony Giddens, another widely cited scholar of modernity, refers to this as a "compression of time." This compression occurs whenever people interact but are actually absent in time (communicating asynchronously) or space (communicating from a distance). Compressed time is what creates our sense of global, supranational community (Giddens 1991).

But Castells prefers to make digital media part of the very definition of our contemporary sense of time. Today, people in network societies use digital media to manage and process information. Some kinds of mediated communications are synchronized, others occur asynchronously. Some cultural products are very fleeting social experiences, yet others are digitally archived. *Timeless time is our sense that past and future converge in the present because digital media bring us things that have already happened and allow us to immediately experience culture produced far away. In Castells' words, it is the disruption of our "biological sense of time as well as logical sequences of time."*

One of the consequences of timeless time is for the space in which communities live. Money is an expression of value, so what does it mean for communities if the things they value are instantly traded with communities on other continents? Digital media unite different communities in their economic, political, and cultural functioning. In other words, the passage of time is less socially relevant because messages arrive so quickly after they are sent. If the owners of a factory sited in your town do not live in the town, and may never even visit the town, much less meet their employees, then what sensibly constitutes the business is the social ties that bind owners with employees and equipment. Place—and the physical community of the town—does not contain the business. Indeed, few physical places contain business the way they once did.

COSMOPOLITAN CULTURE AND CULTURAL IDENTITY

Many observers have commented that the irony of globalization is in raising the prominence of locality as a form of widely recognized cultural content. For the modern, cosmopolitan citizen, physical location no longer predicts cultural tastes. The space of flows allows the resident of Bologna, Fremantle, and Lethbridge to be aware of the latest rap music from Lebanon and the process by which civet coffee is made in Indonesia. In some ways, the mobile phone is a more important digital medium than the computer. A larger number of people have one, and it is the digital medium that we keep with us for most of the waking day. Almost every major software application comes with a mobile version. It is the prime example of technology convergence. In some countries most people have only basic communication services. But even in these countries, the mobile phone is the device for moving around small amounts of money and credit, getting public health updates, and trading jokes with family and friends.

Along with the diffusion of mobile phones, the transformation of cultural industries has afforded many people the opportunity to take control of their identity by more directly managing their cultural consumption. When they do so, argues Castells, people tend to construct their identity based on the specific social networks they inhabit rather than general cultural categories. It is a complex process that allows us to be much more deliberative about how we produce and consume cultural content, because digital media force us to make editorial choices for ourselves. In other words, whereas broadcast media reinforced large-scale cultural categories such as nationalism, religion, or race, digital media allow us to compose our own cultural identity with combinations of content from the global and local networks with which we feel affinity.

Different theorists have used different words to understand what culture is when we as individuals make it with ingredients from global and local sources. Saskia Sassen writes of the "global assemblages" of culture that simultaneously draw content and practices from sources that are simultaneously immediate and local, past and distant (Sassen 2006). Ulrich Beck argues that globalization has brought about a community of social actors who value democratic culture and identify themselves as citizens of the world (Beck 2006). For Castells, it is digital media networks that allow people to assemble these communities of identity.

Of the many kinds of cultural affiliations we can have, nationalism may be the most affected—and most weakened— in the digital media environment. The authority and wealth of the nation-state has been somewhat undermined by global economic power. And recall from the chapter on politics that key to Castells' argument is the point that in most domestic settings, political power is increasingly centered in and exercised in the media. "Why salute the Spanish flag instead of the Catalan flag," opines Castells, "if the armed forces take their orders from American NATO commanders?" (Castells 2000b, 116). With the declining aura of nationalism and digital media that allow us to explore other histories and cultures, other identities rise in prominence.

One of the most important sources of identity, for many people, is their work. In the network society, much employment is found through social networks in businesses that are networked organizations. This means that young people, especially if they are working in cultural industries, are likely to be deeply immersed in work cultures. Particularly in dot-com startups and media businesses, the work week is much longer than average, the distinction between work and non-work time is blurry, and burnout rates are high.

Herein lies an important link between Castells' contemporary research on the media and his early research on the city. Glocalization is a cultural process driven and mediated by powerful cities. Saskia Sassen argues that cities exert enormous strategic control over the rest of the world, because so many key corporate service centers are based in major urban centers (Sassen 2001). She suggests that this can make physical space even *more* important in the modern economy of culture, since it is the headquarters of large corporations sited in London, New York, and Tokyo that have the computational facility to manage global exchanges. These three cities have great concentrations of corporate centers. Other cities may have a few corporate centers, and it is from these centers that global culture is managed. Castells' perspective on space does not place as much emphasis on what is locally sited. For him, spaces are important for what streams through them—the traffic of people and electrons always pass through such nodes on their way across a network.

While cities may be the important nodes through which culture forms and flows, we must turn to one of Castells' colleagues from Paris to understand the role of symbols in identity formation. Baudrillard argued that culture takes the form of systems of signs working together, and that cultural objects only have value in reference to each other. These systems allow people to define themselves by defining who they are not. Moreover, Baudrillard developed the argument that the distinction between real and virtual made little sense because a particular object's cultural value is only understandable through shared images and signs. Power, for Baudrillard, uses the media to ensure that the real no longer exists. Some believe the second Gulf War was about fighting for human rights, others believe it was about searching for weapons of mass destruction, others believe it was about stabilizing fuel supplies. A large portion of the U.S. public believes weapons of mass destruction were found in Iraq, and a large portion of the U.S. public believes President Obama is Muslim. Thus the second Gulf War symbolizes very different things to people who ascribe to different political identities. While Baudrillard did develop his own arguments on the power of the media, he did not make any special distinction between the role of mass media and digital media in symbolic exchange (Merrin 2005).

In contrast to Baudrillard's understanding of how mass media broadcast messages, Castells more specifically argues that digital media afford the power to put ideas and symbols most directly into people's heads. While broadcast media distribute generalized messages, network media narrowcast messages such that they come with the additional credibility of having been sourced by family and friends. Social networks can protect us from contrarian information because we inherently trust our own strong and weak ties—or at least we are well equipped to evaluate the information that comes from our strong and weak ties. So digital media allow for a kind of symbolic violence, by which Castells means "the capacity of a given symbolic code to delete a different code from the individual brain upon whom power is exercised" (Castells 2000a, 8).

The process by which we build a cultural identity in the network society is complex. In some ways we exercise more agency than in the mass media era, because we can actively use digital media to source information from around the global network. We can build transnational identities when we find common cause with social movements around the world, or develop interesting culinary, musical, or literary tastes. But the same social networks that allow us to explore other cultures also bound and bind our explorations. Once we assign our filters—which can be software code or people in the network we trust—we make certain sources a mandatory point of passage for new information. In other words, we can use digital media to become more cosmopolitan and partake in the global space of economic, political, and cultural flows. But codifying our preferences in software may calcify our identity.

MOBILE POLITICS

The internet and mobile phones have helped speed up the news cycle, and improved the informational resources available to investigative journalists and investigative citizens alike. The newly mobile space of flows, however, does not just have economic consequences. The multiple modes of network access also have considerable implications for the business of media politics.

First, mobile phones have become a politically relevant medium, being used to coordinate public protest from Moscow to Tehran. Citizens use mobile phones with cameras to record incidents of fraud at voting stations and to trade jokes about the political candidates they like and dislike. And in most countries with elections, it is hard to imagine a competitive candidate for high-level political office *not* having a mobile or social networking strategy.

Second, with news agencies eager for stories (especially sensational ones) 24 hours a day, new kinds of people and organizations have the opportunity to set a political agenda and frame current affairs. For example, in Spain, Brazil, and

Argentina, average citizens with cheap consumer electronics, lobbyists for small corporations, and foreign governments have all contributed to the shaping of political discourse during elections. This means a lot of new opportunities for non-traditional actors to become media outlets and brokers— they are nodes in media networks that broker information the way editors do. The mobile citizen produces, consumes, and brokers news.

Third, mobile citizens challenge the assumptions of research into public opinion formation. Even if you do not accept the network perspective, this is what makes it exciting to study the media now: simple assertions of clean distinctions between journalist and news consumer no longer hold. Politics, entertainment, and everyday life are not mutually exclusive categories of content. And the time and place of news consumption—or space of flows in Castells' words— are not easily controlled or predicted. The real consequence of the new mobility of communication is that you are now deeply embedded in the networks that produce news.

The modern political protest is an example of the new mobility in the circulation of people, technologies, and ideas. In the summer of 2009, hundreds of thousands of Iranians protested stolen elections. They used Twitter to broadcast stories of police violence; they used their mobile phones to warn each other of the movements of the regime's *Basij* militias. Once the regime caught on to the use of mobile technologies by its opponents, they attempted to use them for counter-insurgency tactics or to disable them altogether. But doing so brought in a cadre of international volunteers who used their information technologies to mirror local content, provide server support to local protest leaders, and supply the international news media with images and stories.

Authoritarian states have long been able to control fixed media infrastructure: they can power down relay stations, burn television stations, and seize supplies of newsprint and ink. Mobile and social media, however, have proven much more difficult for authoritarian regimes to control (Howard 2010). Iran's ruling elites did not fall, but the country's spiritual leaders are split over the regime's tough response, and the protests lasted much longer and had much more international attention than they had the last time an election was rigged.

THE MOBILE IS THE SOCIAL

Castells' work on mobile phones and social media is not as fully developed as the arguments he made based on his study of the first decade of internet development. But the real test of ideas is their applicability to important new phenomena, and many of the things Castells observed about the internet and social organization hold true for other digital media, such as mobile phones and social networking applications. Core to Castells' sense of why media is important is his observation of the ways that power is located and used. For Castells, societies exist by creating a public space in which private interests can be negotiated, collective projects determined, and decisions taken about the common good. In the industrial society, this public space took the (ideal) form of the institutions of the nation-state: democratic elections, an independent judiciary, and an independent civil society.

In the network society, media networks provide the fundamental infrastructure for this public space. And it is social networking software and mobile phones that are the final pieces of technology that allow even the most diffuse subnetworks to hook up to the network society. Compared to the public sphere that Habermas described, this public sphere is structured very differently. It is not just networked and digital, but it is also mobile.

For Castells, digital media bring countries and cultures together in a 24-hour communicative network. The structure of this public sphere is not politically neutral; it is imbued with competing values. The media elites, who are powerful because they produce copyrighted cultural content and own much of the information infrastructure, compete with you as an individual. As an individual, you are powerful because you manage your own information filters and control the final end-point of social communication and cultural consumption (your mobile phone and your computer). As you move through a social world you remain connected to a deeply personal technology. "Multiculturalism is a norm," writes Castells, "rather than the exception in our world" (Castells 2009, 124).

6

CONCLUSION—MEDIA RULES AND
THE RULES OF MEDIA

Digital media now provide the infrastructure in which power is centered, where ideological competition and conflict occurs, and through which physical conflict is coordinated, recorded, and represented. Whereas nation-states used to be the dominant social organization that concentrated power and managed resources, Castells find this power located in media networks. Knowledge is far more central to power than military might. Why has power migrated into media networks? "For one simple reason," writes Castells. "Only at this point in history was a techno-logical infrastructure available to make it possible" (Carnoy and Castells 2001, 3).

The contemporary infrastructure of power certainly includes fast transportation networks for people, goods, and services. But much of the infrastructure of power is in digital media networks: computer systems, advanced tele-communications, and content producers that allow for the management of complex, distributed, networked resources.

People who can create new networks, or who appear as informational brokers across networks of networks, have immense power. Castells' crucial intervention in media research has been to demonstrate the way in which digital technologies are not just infrastructure, but social structure.

This concluding chapter ends with several observations. First, Castells' work on media networks can have an impact on our own sense of how to manage our media networks, and how we use digital media in our daily lives. The chapter will also work to situate readers in their own network society, by offering examples of patterns of technology use and social phenomena that have a direct impact on their lives. Second, the network perspective has clear implications for how we do research on the media. Finally, the chapter introduces some of the most important criticisms of Castells' work on the media. The goal here is not to dismantle his important contributions, but to illustrate some of the lively debates in media research and indentify some of the interesting questions that still need to be answered. By introducing some of the critical responses to Castells' work, the conclusion will also offer some possible directions for future research in media studies. It should also give readers the sense that this is an active and contested domain of inquiry.

THE PERSONAL AND GLOBAL CONTEXTS OF NETWORKS

Whether or not you fully accept a network perspective on media power, there are several basic conclusions you could draw about how to make yourself a secure, sophisticated citizen. If Castells can teach us about how power works in the network society, we can use his observations to both protect us from the abuse of network power and learn how to project network power when we have a cause worthy of doing so.

First, be aware of the "data shadow" you leave as you move through digital networks. Key to the network power of media is the information we leave behind us as we produce and consume digital content. We do not always appreciate how much can be inferred about our attitudes and behavior from the shadow of data we cast as we move through the network society. Recall the three fundamental assumptions of the network perspective: we live in networks made up of nodes of people, technologies, and artifacts; the patterns of links are as important as the nodes themselves; the overall structure provides both capacity for and constraints on action. The server log files, online profiles, credit card histories, medical records, survey responses, and other data we generate are used by others to identify the nodes in our network and to study our relationships. The data is used to manage our opportunities for action by shaping media content, influencing our vote, and encouraging us to buy consumer goods. Purchasing contraceptives on your credit cards (or not having electronic records of such purchases) makes you interesting to the pro-choice lobby (or the pro-life lobby). Subscribing to certain magazines helps advertisers slot you into a market segment that will help them sell you other lifestyle products.[13] Being aware of how your data shadow is a source of power for others gives you some control—in Castells' terms, it gives you counter-power.

Recently, both Google and Facebook have come under significant criticism for how they take care of personal information. Many digital media services, including those offered by Facebook, assume by default that information about users should be made available to Facebook's advertising customers. Google's street mapping project, once heralded as a creative and ambitious attempt to capture images of major urban thoroughfares, inadvertently collected information about people's home Wi-Fi networks. These firms profit by marshaling large volumes of data. They also profit from users who may not like what is done with personal information but who are unwilling or unable to easily "opt-out."

Second, rely on diverse networks for news and information. People who are most likely to get political news and information from similar places in a network should find more diverse ways of getting their news. For example, in 2004, two-thirds of Fox News viewers believed the U.S. had found clear evidence in Iraq that Saddam Hussein was working closely with the al-Qaeda terrorist organization, one-third had thought the U.S. has found weapons of mass destruction in Iraq, and one-third thought the majority of people in the world favored the U.S. invasion of Iraq. Some viewers of other news sources made the same mistakes during the survey, but this misinformation was most pronounced among Fox News viewers (Kull, Ramsay, and Lewis 2003). In a different survey, those who reported getting their news online demonstrated relatively high levels of political sophistication in recognizing political figures and important events (Pew Research Center for the People and the Press 2007). Be critical of the sources of news and information in your life, and try to have several. You may not even need to consume more news, just use social networking applications, the internet, and mobile technologies to keep on top of several networks of opinion.

Third, be aware of how the network perspective itself can be used and misused by political elites. The "network" concept itself was appropriated by the Bush Administration in the United States—and then echoed by the press—for use as a narrowly defined, onerous, and insidious organizational form synonymous with Islamic dissidents (Stohl and Stohl 2007). For these policy makers, networks were treated as information systems for uniplex and ahistorical social relations that were hierarchically organized, top-down command and control structures, with globalized reach connecting homophilous groups. Most important, this orientalized version of network theory stipulated that specifying the boundaries of networks would reveal politically meaningful relations. In contrast, research on network dynamics has demonstrated their multifaceted nature as communication systems. The network form of organization is held together by historically constructed—and limited—relations that allow for dynamic, emergent, adaptive, and flexible associations. Ultimately networks are constructed from other heterogeneous networks that can be described as local and global, or both (Stohl and Stohl 2007). By using the network metaphor in these unusual ways, the crucial conduit of modern terrorist networks is the internet, which in the initial reaction to 9/11 was quickly characterized as the fundamental infrastructure of anti-Western, Islamic fundamentalist activity.

Finally, be aware of your own position in digital networks. The network society is unevenly distributed, and other people have different positions in the network. At a personal level, this means that not everyone will share your level of technological sophistication or your technology habits. Social context may determine the norms of technology use— many of us feel that using a mobile phone in class, on buses, or in planes is obnoxious, a few people do not. Globally, this means that people in other cultures will have slightly different technology habits, and that many will have very little access to digital media. Social inequality can be perpetuated through networks.

Moreover, you are an information broker for other people, so be aware of how your wall posts, tweets, and other digital output may have an impact in your networks. Be aware that people in other countries will have different ways of writing email and may not interpret your messages as you expect. Be

aware that access to information and communication technologies is one of the luxuries that you have, living in one of
the cores of the network society. But not everyone lives in
the core of the network society.

SCIENTIFIC INQUIRY IN THE NETWORK SOCIETY

Castells has had an important influence on media research.
He has significantly advanced our understanding of the
political economy of the network society and our understanding of the power of media. He has always encouraged
his colleagues and students to "use theory, but not let theory
use you." To this end, the network perspective on the way
we study the media both reveals the ways in which expertise
has been used to serve power, the way in which the media
has a role in managing scientific knowledge, and the way in
which new technologies have helped decentralize the means
by which social science is done and disseminated.

Along with encouraging his students to advance research
on power, networks, and the media, Castells offers the critical insight that the media has a significant role in managing
scientific knowledge. Scientific knowledge used to be largely
advanced and controlled by the state, and such knowledge
was often used by the state to reproduce social inequality
(Carnoy and Castells 2001). Scientific research was especially
supported when new investigations offered some promise of
extending the power of the state.

Not only do digital media help disseminate scientific
knowledge to non-experts, but the internet infrastructure
helps decentralize the production of new knowledge. First,
the plethora of open source tools, creative visualization software, and free applications make it possible for average users
to manage and analyze vast amounts of data in a collaborative

manner. Second, the management of scientific inquiry itself is no longer bundled with state power—it resides within the media. "The near-ubiquity of personal computers and internet access in the developed countries is gradually making it possible to access education, particularly at the university level, through privately financed and managed courses of study, many of them promising better training in globally-valued knowledge than provided by the state educational system" (Carnoy and Castells 2001, 10). Finally, even though the internet was originally developed by the United States through a program to network university and military computers, new infrastructure innovations now come from private industry around the world.

There are several good examples of how the internet has become important in the diffusion of scientific knowledge and the arbitration of controversy. Perhaps the best examples are domains of inquiry where the public is presented with the appearance of scientific controversy where none exists. Under the guise of wanting to represent diverse opinions, naysayers of human-induced climate change may be given equal representation with those representing the scientific consensus that global warming is caused by our economic activity. Similarly, creationism may be presented on an equal footing with evolution because it is a competing analytical frame, even though there is widespread scientific consensus behind the general principles of evolution. Doing so may be justified by the media networks as a fair and balanced way to present scientific knowledge to the public. But doing so also serves the media by turning what is not an important scientific controversy into a sensational political controversy.

Aside from the role of news media in covering science, digital networks have had both positive and negative consequences for scientific inquiry. Decentralized knowledge production has resulted in some impressive accomplish-ments, such as Wikipedia and software for dedicating personal computing resources for large networked science projects.[14] Yet hypertext also affects how we learn. Research on how scholars search and cite sources finds that as more journal issues came online, the articles referenced tended to be more recent, fewer journals and articles were cited, and more of those citations were to fewer journals and articles (Evans 2008).

CRITICAL RESPONSES AND ALTERNATIVE APPROACHES

This book is dedicated to what we do get from Castells' network perspective on the media, but there certainly are critical responses to his work. Here we must situate Castells in the broader network of media researchers by identifying the responses to his work and the things a network per-spective does not do well. First, some experts interpret the same trends and evidence that Castells uses in very different ways. Second, for some analysts, Castells does not offer very clear causal explanations and strong arguments about which inputs brought about which outcomes. Third, while Castells claims an interest in network relations, he doesn't formally model these with social network analysis. Finally, even if the causal connections, evidence interpretation, and descriptions of network relations are acceptable, Castells' findings may be best suited for understanding social life in the wealthy urban centers of the West. In other words, he spends more time analyzing evidence from the United States and Europe—core cultures—than in investigating peripheries and non-Western cultures.

The first critique of Castells' work on the media is often made by disagreeing with his interpretation of evidence. In a sense, the challenge of developing grand theory is that describing the analytical frame must have precedence over offering volumes of evidence. Castells admits as much when he says "[I offered] illustrations of an analytical point I was trying to communicate, not evidence" (Castells 1999, 294). This means that if we find some of his conclusions intuitively sensible, there is plenty of work to be done collecting large amounts of evidence in a purposeful way to make the conclusions convincing.

In Castells' work, new information technology is one of the causes of globalization, but globalization has also brought about the new information technologies. And the autonomy of the state has declined as power finds a more effective home in media networks than in the institutions of the judiciary, military, or government. But some historians would argue that the state has never been very autonomous and always been embedded in a social context with other civic and religious institutions. Some political scientists would say the state is still quite capable of acting autonomously. The state has hardly been "phased out" and, since information management has always been important, its bureaucratic form has really just been transformed. States are still decisive and aggressive institutions, especially in times of economic or political crisis, and very little global information infrastructure is built without state investment and oversight.

In the realm of political life, it is hard to find major political candidates who are only "internet candidates." In other words, there are a few examples of networked campaigns that managed to get their issues onto the national agenda or get their candidates into office. But most electoral and legislative victories in most countries are still determined by campaign contributions and the charisma of civic leaders—not by the number of campaign friends on a social networking site. Radical public policy alternatives may become popular among networks of like-minded individuals. But without pickup by the major news organizations, being a good idea is not enough. So there are some examples of media power over networks, but in important ways, it is politics as usual.

In addition, there is evidence that all the new information-tion technologies and networking tools have had very little impact on political sophistication. In the United States, it seems that the average adult is about as unable to name their leaders and is about as unaware of international affairs and major news events as 20 years ago. This is despite the greater diversity in the variety of news programming available on cable networks, the increased interactivity of news websites, and rising levels of education (Pew Research Center for the People and the Press 2007).

One of Castells' important contributions has been the notion that economic, political, and cultural power no longer really resides in the state, and instead resides in media networks dominated by such firms as Disney and Time Warner or such people as Rupert Murdoch and Silvio Berlusconi. But it may be a contradiction to also argue that power resides in the diversity and largely autonomous origin of content from individual users who are globally distributed and globally interactive. Is power closely held by media monopolies or widely distributed among increasingly sophisticated citizens?

It may actually be that there are several kinds of power, held by different actors. Castells offers a distinction between power and counter-power, the latter being the ability to challenge domination and equalize social relations. There are, however, very few good examples of social movements successfully using their counter-power to achieve major changes in political institutions. Certainly there are many small examples of innovative campaigns and singular victories on particular issues by figures outside the mainstream. There may be a few small examples of what Castells calls counter-power when networked citizens use digital media in creative ways in the cause of social justice. But it is hard to add up these few examples and conclude that the public sphere has been changed forever.

Entrenched political interests are good at co-opting challengers and learning new tricks. Disney and Time Warner still produce the vast majority of our cultural content. Berlusconi is still effectively managing Italy and Murdoch's media empire is expanding into the developing world. Most citizens get their news from the television, and only interact with political news and information at election time.

The second critique of Castells' work is that he rarely offers clear causal connections. When and where did the network society begin? It is tough to answer this, because as Castells admits, new technologies always have their precedents and their developments. The first designs of a network linking university and military computer installations emerged around 1969, fiber optic cable was designed around 1971, and microcomputers were commercially available by the end of the 1970s. But the most important parts of internet infrastructure in the U.S. were not privatized until 1995. The network enterprise developed most quickly during the dot-com boom at the turn of the century. Many of today's network devices—which have an impact on the space of flows—were not commercially available until 2005. And broadband technologies, which are needed to rapidly distribute larger amounts of content more quickly, are still concentrated in the wealthy countries of the northern hemisphere. Even if a new technological paradigm—as Castells puts it—evolved in the early 1970s, it was 30 years before the social changes he labels as features of a network society materialized.

The network perspective may not reveal clear sources of agency and clear lines of causality. Castells often claims that the network society was born of the social movements that emerged in the 1960s in the United States and Western Europe. It may be true that these movements preceded the digital media by a decade, but that is not a sufficient causal story. These movements are not usually held up as examples of highly networked social movements (many consider the Zapatistas the earliest and best example of a new media social movement). It may be that some of the people who participated in these movements went on to design and use digital media, imbuing technology with their democratic values, but others have fully developed that argument (Turner 2006).[15] How is it helpful to have a macro theory of social change that situates media as the cause of both centralized and decentralized power?

The third critique of Castells' use of network theory is that he does not do formal modeling of networks. Many of the political scientists, sociologists, and communication researchers who do social network analysis have a highly evolved mathematical language for studying ties and nodes. There are fairly easy calculations that can be done to compute the size of a network. Boundaries, centrality, and other network properties can be defined in very precise scientific terms (Monge and Contractor 2003). Yet Castells does not use these analytical tools, even though his research questions suggest that social network analysis would help him strengthen his arguments. Castells' method, even though he is concerned with communication networks, is more akin to a general approach to political economy.

A final critique is that most of the good analysis Castells does seems to be based on evidence that comes from the wealthy countries of North America and Europe. Much of what Castells studies is at the core of networks, and much of his evidence comes from global cities, the major media organizations in the United States and Europe, and the wealthy countries of the West. Castells offers, perhaps, less insight into the impact of digital media on the rest of the world. Many developing countries had very different mass media systems from those of the West, with tight control of television and radio broadcasts but very vibrant print media. There are several ways in which Castells' theory does not travel well. Does Castells' perspective on the network society really travel well outside of the United States and Europe? Do conclusions drawn with evidence from New York, Los Angeles, and London hold true when applied to Windhoek, Colombo, and Dushanbe?

In important ways understanding the core of global communication networks reveals much about power and by definition helps us understand what is not happening at the periphery of communication networks. But, when it comes to media and information, technical literacy as well as general literacy varies quite a bit from country to country. Media diets are different in Africa, Latin America, and Southeast Asia, where print newspapers are still a dominant political institution. Yet the analysis of life on the periphery of media networks is not just about developing countries, it is about sources of social inequality in developed countries too.

Networks have boundaries, and there are known ways that networks perpetuate inequality. The urban poor in Marseilles, Chicago, and Mexico City share the feature of having less social or cultural capital than wealthy elites. Or at the very least, the urban poor have specific kinds of social and cultural capital that do not directly provide job mobility and easy improvements to their quality of life. If such communities are also on the periphery of media networks and internet access is a luxury, their experience of the network society must be very different from ours. Most of the stories that Castells tells about transformative moments and hierarchical institutions apply most obviously in Europe, the United States, and a few other global cities. Would his arguments fall apart, or be stronger, if he more aggressively sought evidence from the developing world?

Castells' network perspective on the media does not convince everyone. For some media experts, his approach does not offer clear causal pathways, exclusive ways of interpreting evidence, formal social network analysis, or life on the periphery of the network society. There are others who have advanced the network perspective and describe the network society in other ways. Van Dijk, one of the first to develop a comprehensive definition of a network society, places less emphasis on the transformative role of digital media. Capitalism and patriarchy are such long-standing institutional forms that information and communication technologies are only weak sources of power. Indeed, for van Dijk, it is much more likely that capitalism will reshape technologies to serve its goals (van Dijk 2006). But what unites many of the scholars who use the concept of a network society is the conviction that digital media have helped social networks become one of the primary organizational forms across many different economic, political, and cultural institutions.

REMAINING QUESTIONS AND FUTURE DIRECTIONS OF RESEARCH

One of the challenges of developing big-picture, all-encompassing theories is that it can be difficult to identify specific causal linkages. Some empirical evidence seems tentative or thin. Even though Castells' work on the media, and the network perspective generally, is widely respected, there remain important questions that should inspire future research. The new generation could work on the areas that Castells' critics have already identified as missing in a network perspective.

Most contemporary research on the media and society either critiques Castells' ideas, or is in dialogue with them. Manuel Castells' contribution has been to offer unique insights, but also to inspire new questions. Causal paths are most difficult to identify when the consequences are far-ranging. So what is new? Castells is at his best when answering this question.

> What is new is the capacity to link up global financial markets around the clock around the world, with the processing information capacity to shift billions of dollars back and forth in seconds between countries, markets, and complex financial products. What is new is the capacity to integrate management, production, and distribution through the planet without losing focus and coordination. What is new is the capacity to launch instant air-based wars with precision strikes, increasingly by automatic systems. What is new is a global media system, able at the same time to connect the audiences of the whole world to one single broadcast, and to customize messages to a specific audience in a given locality. What is new is the internet as the system of horizontal, global, relatively unimpeded, interactive communication in chosen time. (Castells 2000b, 113)

In important ways, Castells may still share some of Marx's dialectical materialism. Castells is still very interested in material relations between people and organizations. And one of the core assumptions in his work is that the network society will eventually come to every community. His perspective on the media is that the periphery of the network society is still linked to the global core of communication networks. And, the pace at which local organizational forms will give way to network forms seems unstoppable.

The work of observing social change is not done, though it might be advanced with his analytical frame on the media. There are limits to empirical science that must move forward through observation without experimental controls. But the next generation of media scholars will certainly be influenced by what Manuel Castells has observed.

Castells' thinking has evolved over time. His later works are confident statements that the network society is an important theoretical paradigm worth taking seriously. His earlier works, however, propose that the network society is but one structural element of information societies or the information age. Eventually he discards these monikers of information societies and information ages for that of the network society. He finds solid theoretical footing in the empirical research that went into the three-volume *The Information Age* and *Communication Power*. A reductive way to evaluate a researcher—or an analytical frame—is in terms of strengths or weakness. But it may be more meaningful to evaluate Castells' contributions in terms of what you get and what you do not get, or what you see and what you do not see, with his network perspective on the media. Two additional domains of future research include study of how media networks impact social inequality, and how these networks impact the practice of religion.

As a scholar aware of his political roots, Castells has made the study of social inequality in the network society a crucial domain of inquiry. But with the ever-changing technologies that form the infrastructure of the network society, fresh research on how such inequality is preserved or overcome is always valued. What impact do global networks have on social inequality? Recall that network relations tie global cities together, and bind multinational firms in relations of production and consumption. The concept of the space of flows was used to introduce Castells' notions on cultural production, but this concept is also relevant for understanding concentrations of wealth and distributions of poverty. The global connections of financial centers do not simply connect Mexico City, Brasilia, and Rio de Janeiro with Madrid, Barcelona, and Milan. It is the central business districts that are connected in the global space of financial flows. Around each of these central business districts are neighborhoods largely excluded from powerful network relations.

> I propose the notion of the emergence of a Fourth World of exclusion, made up not only of most of Africa and rural Asia, and of Latin American shanties, but also of the South Bronx, La Courneuve, Kamagasaki, or Tower Hamlets of this world. A fourth world that is predominantly populated by women and children. (Castells 1997, 8)

How do networks help structure poverty? What are the barriers to entering the media-rich world that many of us live in? What would new technologies of empowerment look like?

In the realm of culture and identity, the role of religion in the network society needs further research. Do media networks homogenize cultures, or play a role in one faith's dominance over another? If global media is the new home of social power, will religious institutions suffer the same fate as the nation-state, becoming secondary sources of affiliation? When do organized religions use networks to extend their reach, and under which conditions are they successful? If religious extremists are in the minority, will networks amplify their message and their ability to recruit new members, or will networks of tempered, non-violent faithful relegate extremists to the most marginal subnetworks of society? Castells' research on the media has inspired a generation of scholars. Yet there is inspiration enough for further work: "theory is simply a research tool," he writes, "not the end product of research" (Castells 2000a, 6).

THE NEW POWER OF DIGITAL MEDIA

As you are reading this book, the number of people who have ever used the internet is hitting two billion. How have digital media, like the internet, had an impact on all these people? A network perspective on studying the media reveals the ways in which linkages provide structure. From a network perspective, the media rule social life. "Media" must be understood broadly: it includes the information infrastructure that supports network enterprises and the global economy; it includes the digital content about politicians and public policy options that we evaluate at election time; it includes the industries that produce video games, the temporary production teams that give us movies, and the tools that allow creative individuals to produce cultural content at home.

Today, we live in a society that is informational, global, and networked. It is informational in that generating knowledge and managing information makes or breaks the modern firm, determines whether political candidates or social movements succeed or fail, and whether cultural icons propagate or fade from memory. It is global in that the core political, economic, and cultural processes work on a planetary scale in real time or chosen time. It is networked in that communication technologies connect firms or segments of firms in project-based work, important political actors battle for power over media 24 hours a day, and cultural production increasingly involves digitally networked media while interest in cultural products spreads through networks of family and friends (Castells 2000a).

Media provides the rules of social interaction, it is where we find power concentrated and exercised, it is what we use to build social capital for ourselves, and it is what we use to spend that social capital over our life course. Digital media provide not just the infrastructure, but the structure, of our social lives.

APPENDIX

There are several ways to explore your own networks and your own media consumption habits. Since so much of the media we consume is digitally produced and digitally consumed, and since so many of us use digital media to manage our social networks, data on both can be easy to collect. These exercises use a network perspective to reveal, in a personal and immediate way, something about how social life is constructed. The first exercise allows readers to map their own social networks by using data from their mobile phones, Facebook profile, or personal calendar. The second exercise allows readers to track their exposure to digital media through a time diary, and reveals the varied ways in which network communication technologies structure the cultural content of their lives. These exercises will allow you to relate to the more abstract notions of the network society. For the exercises to work well, follow the directions carefully but be thoughtful and creative in telling stories from your data. Building a sensible narrative from data is the key task in social research.

AN EXERCISE IN VISUALIZING YOUR OWN
DIGITAL NETWORKS

We often visualize our social relations as lists: alphabetically in computer programs of contacts, or by priority of who has called us most recently on our mobile phone. And when we think about our friends and families, it is natural to organize them into different groups related to the different communities we inhabit. But a fundamental assumption of the network perspective is that even though we tend to think in groups, we are actually in networks. So what does your social network look like?

These exercises will have you extract data about your social network from Facebook, Twitter, your mobile phone, or some other digital media. You will produce a network map based on this data, and the goal of the exercise is to understand the scope of our online social networks as they become an increasingly influential part of our generation's culture and to gain familiarity with tools that can interact with new media and utilize these tools to analyze data in a social context. The first method will result in a detailed network map of your closest associations; the second will reveal a much larger network structure of your relationships.

A Small, Purposive Sample, Analyzed by Hand

First, make a list of 10 names, but collect the names in some purposefully sampled way from the digital media you use in your daily life. You could check your mobile phone and use the last 10 people to call you or the first 10 entries, alphabetically by last name. If you have a blog or social networking profile, you could take the last 10 people who commented on one of your posts, or the first 10 people you linked up to. Alternatively, you could use the last 10 people to send you an email or look at your list of contacts and choose your 10 closest friends. Think about the implications of how you sample, because they way you pull out names will have an impact on what you learn about the structure of your social life. But also don't overthink your sampling strategy, because the goal here is just to conceptualize the structure of links between a small group of other people, not your entire social network.

Second, sketch out a network diagram of how you are linked to these people, and how they may be linked to each other. Use a pencil and several blank sheets of paper to conceptualize your network. In your first draft, write your name at the center of the page, and write the other 10 names around the edge of the page. These people are nodes in your network, and each node will have at least one dyadic relationship—a tie to you. Then connect all the nodes to you, using different kinds of lines to represent the nature of the tie. Begin simply, by drawing strong and weak ties using thick and thin lines. Since all of these people are friends of different strengths, make a strong tie for friends you've known for more than a year, and a weak tie for new friends, whom you only met in the last year. It is possible that you will be the only person linking any two of the other people in the network, but it is more likely that some of them know each other quite well, and don't need you as a broker for their relationship. You may have to guess at how strong or weak the tie between other people is, but do your best.

There are many ways to present this network information, so have several sheets of paper ready to sketch different possibilities. Some versions of your network map will work better than others. For example, the width of lines could be directly related to the number of minutes you spent talking to each person over the last week using your mobile phone, or the number of emails you have traded this month. Or you use dotted lines to represent family connections—we don't choose our family—and solid lines to represent ties to friends.

You could also use color to distinguish workplace ties from family, school, and friendship ties. Or colors could be used to distinguish relevant demographic features of people in their network, such as gender, race, or age. Colors could also be associated with types of digital media. Do you use a mobile phone to communicate with family, but text messages and social networking software to maintain relationships with your peer group? Ties could also be made directional, especially if you remember who initiated the relationship first, or if you have information about who tends to initiate the majority of phone calls, emails, or text messages. Play with the organization of names. For example, you could use another sheet to organize names into clusters of affiliation. People you know from work could be clustered at the top of the page, people you know from school clustered at the bottom of the page, and everyone else in between. One good combination could be to place your closest friends and relatives near you on the page, use directional ties to reveal who tends to initiate communications most often, and color code the tie by the form of digital media most often used.

Third, make a simple calculation of how dense your network is. Network density is the ratio of actual ties to the total possible number of ties. If everyone in your network is connected to everyone else, the network density would 1.00. Since you chose to map out links to 10 people, there would be at most 110 links. Add up the number of actual links you observed, divide by 110, and this will give you a measure of the network density of your map. A high value reveals a very dense network, a low value reveals a more sparse network. Since you may not know about all the ties between the people in your network, your network may seem sparsely populated.

Finally, sit with the best version of your network map and think about how it may reveal or obscure features of how your life is organized. This particular exercise will probably result in a network map that makes you a very central intermediary for the other nodes in the network. In other words, you broker their relationships, and if they want to develop a social tie to other people in the network they could go through you. Does data collected from digital media offer a good reflection of the social structure in which you live? If you had used data from another medium might something else have been revealed?

A Large Sample, Using Open Source Software

Large network images can reveal more about the overall structure of your affiliations, though with less nuance. Sampling a large part of your network using digital media involves extracting data, describing and visualizing your network, and then developing an analytical narrative about what you've found.

There are several useful programs available for collecting and analyzing data about the relationships you maintain in your digital media. This exercise will have you collect data from your Facebook page with an application called My Online Social Network, and then allow you to use NodeXL, a free plug-in for the PC version of Microsoft Excel, to map your network.

First, go to My Online Social Network (Facebook App) and log in to your account. The site will pull a list of your friends and their relationships with each other. Be patient, if you have a large network it will take the program some time to trace all ties. The resulting data can be saved to your own hard drive, and it will look like a singe column listing your friends, followed by another column of the friends they share with you. Copy and paste all of the Facebook "friend data" into a Word or text-only document, and delete the first few rows of text that don't actually contain friend names. Save this document to your hard drive as a back-up copy of your network data.

Second, download and install the NodeXL application (http://nodexl.codeplex.com/). Note it is an add-on for the PC version of Excel, but may not work in other operating systems. The program creates maps of nodes and ties from two columns of data. Each time two of your friends appear side by side in the same row, the program will draw a line connecting them as nodes. The program automatically groups people who share common friends, so the advantage of using it is that subnetworks you are not really aware of may appear in the map. Follow the instructions for installing NodeXL, and you can use the Excel 2007 template as the basis of your own image. You will see that there are no spaces between a friend's first and last name, but that there are spaces between two different friends. Since these spaces delimit the column of your friends from the column of friends' friends, import the file into Excel and instruct it to use the space as a marker for making different columns in the spreadsheet. When the data has been successfully imported, the data should clearly be organized into different columns.

Within NodeXL, you will notice that column A is your list of friends, but that many of the first rows in column B are empty. As you scroll down column B you will eventually run across names—these are the friends of friends. But to complete the network data you must insert your name into the blank cells in column B. After all, these people are not just nodes in your network; you broker their relationships with other people. So type in your name (no space between first and last name), and then copy and paste that into all the blank cells in column B. This situates you in the network.

The climax comes when you are able to refresh the graph, and have the program map out all of the ties in your network. You can play with the attributes of the graph to bring out particular details. Adjusting the scale will make the individual lines more refined. Go back to the data and play with the color or width of lines to set subnetworks into relief. You are the best person for interpreting the data, because you will spot how networks of high school friends may be different from work colleagues, how family may be networked to each other but not to your friends, or how one or two romantic partners are actually brokers of subnetworks.

These programs are often updated, and there may be new applications for analyzing your social networks. Do not be afraid to explore the latest alternatives, or to play with the process if the steps described above no longer quite apply. Most of the software for analyzing these large social networks is open source and many developers will respond quickly to your questions if you explain what you would like to do with the data. The final step in analyzing your network map, regardless of whether you used the process just described or not, is the most important.

Regardless of your research design, the process of learning about your social network—and the graphic itself—will form the basis of evidence in your personal social network essay. Exposing the different kinds of ties in your network can be interesting enough, but you might also consider using this network map to develop a narrative essay about the structure of your social life. As yourself, how do communication networks provide capacities or constraints on your interactions? What kinds of ties are strong ties, and what kinds are weak ties? This exercise should help you identify the important

people brokering your networks, and the networks you serve
as an important broker.

AN EXERCISE IN TRACKING YOUR MEDIA AND CULTURAL CONSUMPTION

The term "media" is used to refer to many different things,
including hardware, software, television and movies, journalists and Hollywood production companies, video game
designers, art, and many other kinds of cultural industries. A
simple exercise will allow you to track the range of cultural
products you are exposed to over a range of technologies for
delivering those messages. To get a good sample of the range
of media you consume, you will need to plan out the research,
prepare for the study period, keep a diary of the ways in which
you consume culture, and write a short essay on the ways in
which you consume culture over a fixed period of time.

To begin this research, first set an achievable writing goal
and a time frame for data collection. For example, if you
keep track of the kinds of culture you consume in a 24-hour
period, you should be able to write a smart, succinct, 500-
word essay. Commit to the time period of study at least a day
in advance, so that you have time to prepare your methods
of data collection.

Next, prepare for the study period by reflecting on the
ways you are most likely to consume culture. Some ways are
obvious, especially if you have regular television watching
and internet use habits, but some media for cultural content
are less obvious than others:

- Newspapers
- Magazines
- Books
- Radio

- Television
- Film
- Internet
- Mobile phones
- Billboards
- Other people's T-shirts
- Other forms of streaming digital content
- Propaganda posters on telephone poles

Keeping a diary of cultural consumption for a 24-hour period will result in a raw source of data for your essay. Keep a notepad with you all day, and observe the type of media carrying cultural content to you and note the duration of your exposure. Once you have a diary log for a 24-hour period, do some basic research into the organizations—corporate, government, or otherwise—that generated the content that you consumed.

In the beginning of your essay, make some generalization about your media consumption habits. What can we learn about you from the content you consume and your consumption habits? What role does consuming media—watching TV, going to movies, listening to music—play in your world? In the middle of your essay, report some specific calculations and percentages about the amount of time you spend exposed to different media. How much in total of your 24-hour period, how much for particular media, or how much over new media? Are there other interesting trends revealed when you analyze the data about your habits? In your conclusion, assess the organizations that were generating the content you consumed. How do you think the media industry sees you and what would they learn about you from your consumption habits?

You will probably find some surprising things that will make for great analytical observations in your essay. But you will also be able to try your hand at defining some terms or answering some research questions, in a very grounded way, with the evidence from your time diary. What kinds of cultural content are you exposed to most often? Are there any patterns to the messages that seem targeted to your age, gender, race, or ethnicity? Based on your observations, how would you even define culture?

Time diary research is one of the most important methods we have for collecting data about our daily experiences. If done carefully over a short period of time, you can create a great snapshot of the interactions in your life. But because this is self-reported data, the trick is to systematize the way the observations are collected and catalogued. One way of organizing such observations is to devote a small notebook to the entries you make. A small legal pad, blue book (like you use for exams) would work well. Alternatively, you could design your own coding sheet.

For the cultural consumption diary, you should consider collecting similar kinds of information: the location of exposure, the time of day, the duration of exposure, the type of media (TV, poster, radio, etc.), the content of the media (music genre, name of program, message on T-shirt), activity you were engaged while you were exposed (sitting at home, walking down the street), and any interesting observations, feelings, encounters.

This exercise has several goals. First, this exercise will make you critically assess your media use patterns. Second, this exercise will encourage you to develop and practice your writing style. Third, this exercise will encourage you to reflect on how media industries produce content for you. Ask yourself how you can improve the diversity of culture and information you get on a daily basis. This exercise should help you find ways to become a more sophisticated citizen of the network society.

AN EXERCISE IN SURVEILLANCE AND
SOUSVEILLANCE—TRACKING THE TRACKERS

What is surveillance? It may be so omnipresent that we are used to it and now fully aware of what it is and how much it happens. Surveillance is something that political elites, cultural producers, and economic actors do to better understand your attitudes and behavior. Sousveillance is something you can do to better understand the attitudes and behavior of those powerful actors. For example, governments collect vast amounts of information about citizens. But with the network flows of information through nodes like wikileaks, citizens can encounter vast amounts of information about the behavior of their governments.

In this exercise, you will plan out the research, prepare for the study period, keep a diary of the ways in which you are surveilled, and write a short essay on the ways in which you leave a digital trail over a fixed period of time.

First, develop a research plan by setting an achievable writing goal and time frame for data collection. For example, if you keep track of the ways you are surveilled in a 24-hour period, you should be able to write a smart, succinct, 500-word essay. Commit to the time period of study at least a day in advance, so that you have time to organize the ways in which you will collect data.

Second, prepare for the study period by thinking about the ways in which you are likely to expose surveillance, and prepare. Electronic surveillance occurs in obvious ways, from credit card purchases, bank transactions, and email logs. But it also occurs in surreptitious and unexpected ways. Obviously you can't anticipate all of these, but spending some time listing the likely means of digital surveillance will equip you to track the trackers. Means of collecting data about you can include:

- Closed and open-circuit security cameras
- Credit card purchases, both amount spent and particular consumer goods
- Bank machines
- Email logs
- Listening to music online
- Telephone records
- Library bar codes
- Meal cards
- Bus cards
- Highway toll cards
- Supermarket cards
- Website cookies
- Website spy ware

To prepare for the study period, you might make yourself aware of cameras at work or school or public places. If you use the internet a lot, you can install programs that alert you about web bugs, ad networks and widgets on visited web pages. To see how your online activities are being tracked, consider installing a free trial version of one of the many ad-blocking, cookie-detecting software such as Ad-Aware or ZoneAlarm, to see what these programs catch. If you use Firefox, the Ghostery app will reveal which servers are tracking your online movements. Go into your browser and familiarize yourself with your cookie settings. If you flush all the cookies out of your browser at the beginning of the study period, by the end of your study period you will have a fresh list of cookies. There may be other ways of preparing for the study period so that when you are actively collecting data you can make your observations quickly and efficiently.

Your essay will almost read like an entry in a personal diary, though the concluding paragraphs should offer some big-picture analysis or critical commentary on what you've learned. Almost everybody will find something surprising about how they are surveilled—we rarely appreciate the form and extent of digital surveillance.

The surveillance diary will be the raw data source for your essay. Keep a notepad with you specifically for making notes on your data trail; make the notepad a diary of occasions where you noticed surveillance and electronic recording, and note the duration of your exposure. Once you have a diary log for your study period, do some basic research into private companies or government organizations that were collecting data on you. The surveillance diary can be set up much like the cultural consumption diary in the previous exercise. There are several kinds of data points you should consider collecting: the location of surveillance, the time of day surveillance took place, the duration of exposure, the type of surveillance (video, audio, transaction, etc.), what you were doing and how your behavior changed under surveillance, and any interesting observations, feelings, encounters.

In the beginning of your essay, identify the different ways you were surveilled and the kind of data that were collected. In the middle of your essay, write about who collected the data on you, why, and who has access to the data about you. At the end of your essay, speculate about how the surveillance data might be used. In the abstract, what might other people learn about general human behavior from the data? In particular, what might other people learn about you specifically from the data?

This exercise has several goals, the most important of which is to help you realize how much data you generate. Why is privacy valuable to you? You may have the right to be left alone, it might be useful to have fewer intrusions into your life, or you might want to constrain what governments and corporations learn about you. But are there some conditions under which you are willing to sacrifice your privacy?

If you look at the evidence about how people can surveille you or search for information about you, are you satisfied with the trade-offs? First, this exercise will encourage you to be aware of the electronic data trail you leave in an average day through a wide range of technologies. Second, this exercise will encourage you to develop and practice your writing style. Third, this exercise will encourage you to think philosophically and reflectively about what other people can deduce from data about you.

NOTES

1 The National Science Foundation has an informative multimedia presentation on its role in building internet infrastructure: http://www.nsf.gov/news/special_reports/nsf-net/.

2 If you are interested in what the Syrian ruler's Facebook page looks like, see: http://www.facebook.com/pages/Dr-Bashar-Al-Assad-d-bshar-alasd/56730314485?ref=search.

3 If you are interested in the latest information on media ownership, explore the databases at the "State of the Media Project": http://www.stateofthemedia.org/2010/media-owner ship/.

4 To find the Bacon Numbers of other actors, evaluate an actor's links to Sean Connery, or see how other actors are good centers in the Hollywood universe, go to: http://oracle ofbacon.org.

5 For an interesting look at the social networks on film sets, see Bechky (2006).

6 To remix an image of yourself into the ubiquitous poster from the Obama 2008 presidential campaign, see: http://obami conme.pastemagazine.com.

7 Readers in the United States may be interested in using the resources offered by the Center for Responsive Politics

(www.opensecrets.org) to look for networks of power that might involve their own political representatives. Similarly, TheyRule.net is a useful tool for analyzing the network structure of corporate boards of major firms, boards that often employ former politicians.

8 News aggregators are good examples of how digital media create a unique space of flows that brings together cultural content from disparate places and different times to the same place and point in time. For example, see the world's news headlines all in one place at http://www.newseum.org/todays frontpages/ or a ten by ten constructed image of the most important photos appearing on prominent online news sources at http://www.tenbyten.org/.

9 See the latest "Know Your Meme" stream on YouTube.com. Memetic news, delivered in images and keywords, can be calibrated by the hour using http://www.tenbyten.org.

10 *Firefly* is a good example of how conflict can arise between cultural industries used to old models of production and consumers eager to be drawn into the cultural community of the show. The television show's fan base was energized enough to motivate Universal Studios to release the feature-length movie *Serenity*, but then Universal sued fans who produced amateur merchandise and developed digital content outside the studio's purview. Universal Studios wanted guerilla marketing to help promote what they saw as their movie, but also threatened to fine an amateur T-shirt producer with $150,000 per infringed work.

11 The most complex productions include *Star Trek: the New Series*, but others are listed on Wikipedia: http://en.wikipedia. org/wiki/Star_Trek_fan_productions.

12 For more on the space of flows, see Castells 1999 and Chapter 6 of Castells 1996.

13 To find out how your data shadow is used to generate marketing schemes for advertising agencies, see: http://www.claritas. com/MyBestSegments.

14 Readers interested in contributing to networked science projects should consider participating in malaria research (http://www.malariacontrol.net/), contributing a transcript of tapes from the Nixon Whitehouse (http://www.nixontapes.

org/index.htm), or research into the nature of artificial intelligence (http://www.jabberwacky.com/).

15 In the second chapter of *Internet Galaxy*, Castells does argue that the graduate students involved in the earliest stages of internet development imbued an "internet culture" of sharing and cooperation (Castells 2001).

REFERENCES

Anderson, Benedict. 1991. *Imagined Communities: Reflections on the Origin and Spread of Nationalism*. London, UK: Verso.

Anderson, Chris. 2008. *The Long Tail, Revised and Updated Edition: Why the Future of Business is Selling Less of More*. New York, NY: Hyperion.

Aoyama, Yuko, and Manuel Castells. 2002. An empirical assessment of the informational society: Employment and occupational structures of G-7 countries, 1920–2000. *International Labour Review* 141, 1: 123–159.

Appadurai, Arjun. 1996. *Modernity At Large: Cultural Dimensions of Globalization*. Minneapolis, MN: University of Minnesota Press.

Arsenault, Amelia, and Manuel Castells. 2008a. The structure and dynamics of global multi-media business networks. *International Journal of Communication* 2, 1: 707–748.

Arsenault, Amelia, and Manuel Castells. 2008b. Switching power: Rupert Murdoch and the global business of media politics: a sociological analysis. *International Sociology* 23, 4: 488–513.

Bechky, Beth A. 2006. Gaffers, gofers, and grips: Role-based coordination in temporary organizations. *Organization Science* 17, 1: 3–21.

Beck, Ulrich. 2006. *Power in the Global Age: A New Global Political Economy*. Cambridge, UK: Polity.

Benkler, Yochai. 2007. *The Wealth of Networks: How Social Production Transforms Markets and Freedom*. New Haven, CT: Yale University Press.

Bennett, W. Lance. 1990. Toward a theory of press–state relations in the United States. *Journal of Communication* 40, 2: 103–127.

Bourdieu, Pierre. 1987. *Distinction: A Social Critique of the Judgement of Taste*. Cambridge, MA: Harvard University Press.

Cairncross, Frances. 1997. *The Death of Distance: How the Communications Revolution Will Change Our Lives*. Cambridge, MA: Harvard Business Press.

Carnoy, Martin, and Manuel Castells. 2001. Globalization, the knowledge society, and the network state: Poulantzas at the millennium. *Global Networks* 1, 1: 1–18.

Castells, Manuel. 1996. *The Information Age I: The Rise of the Network Society*. Malden, MA: Blackwell Publishers.

———. 1997a. An introduction to the Information Age. *City* 2, 7: 6–16.

———. 1997b. *The Information Age II: The Politics of Identity*. Malden, MA: Blackwell Publishers.

———. 1997c. *The Information Age III: End of Millennium*. Malden, MA: Blackwell Publishers.

———. 1998. A rejoinder: On power, identities and culture in the network society [Book Review]. *New Political Economy* 3, 3: 473–483.

———. 1999. Grassrooting the space of flows. *Urban Geography* 20, 4: 294–302.

———. 2000a. Materials for an explanatory theory of the network society. *British Journal of Sociology* 51, 1: 5–24.

———. 2000b. Globalization and identity in the network society: A rejoinder to Calhoun, Lyon and Touraine. *Prometheus* 4, 1: 107–123.

———. 2000c. Grassrooting the space of flows. In *Cities in the Telecommunications Age: The Fracturing of Geographies*, ed. James Wheeler, Yuko Aoyama, and Barney Warf, 18–27. New York, NY: Routledge.

———. 2001. *The Internet Galaxy: Reflections on the Internet, Business, and Society*. Oxford, UK: Oxford University Press.

————. 2004. Informationalism, networks, and the network society: A theoretical blueprint. In *The Network Society: A Cross-Cultural Perspective*, ed. Manuel Castells, 3–43. New York, NY: Edward Elgar.

————. 2007. Communication, power and counter-power in the network society. *International Journal of Communication* 1, 1: 238–266.

————. 2009. *Communication Power*. New York, NY: Oxford University Press.

————. 2010. The new public sphere: Global civil society, communication networks, and global governance. *The ANNALS of the American Academy of Political and Social Science* 616, 1: 78–93.

Castells, Manuel, and Martin Ince. 2003. *Conversations with Manuel Castells*. Cambridge, UK: Polity.

Castells, Manuel, Imma Tubella, Teresa Sancho, and Barry Wellman. 2003. *The Network Society in Catalonia: An Empirical Analysis*. Barcelona: La Rosa del Vents Mondadori.

Deuze, Mark. 2007. *Media Work*. Oxford, UK: Polity.

Evans, James A. 2008. Electronic publication and the narrowing of science and scholarship. *Science* 321, 5887: 395–399.

Fischer, Claude S. 1994. *America Calling: A Social History of the Telephone to 1940*. Berkeley, CA: University of California Press.

Giddens, Anthony. 1991. *The Consequences of Modernity*, 1st edn. Palo Alto, CA: Stanford University Press.

Gillespie, Tarleton. 2009. *Wired Shut: Copyright and the Shape of Digital Culture*. Cambridge, MA: MIT Press.

Granovetter, Mark. 1973. The strength of weak ties. *American Journal of Sociology* 78, 6: 1360–1380.

Habermas, Jürgen. 1991. *The Structural Transformation of the Public Sphere: An Inquiry into a Category of Bourgeois Society*. Cambridge, MA: MIT Press.

Howard, Philip N. 2010. *The Digital Origins of Dictatorship and Democracy: Information Technology and Political Islam*. New York, NY: Oxford University Press.

Innis, Harold A. 2008. *The Bias of Communication*. 2nd edn. Toronto: University of Toronto Press.

Jenkins, Henry. 2006. *Convergence Culture: Where Old and New Media Collide*. New York, NY: NYU Press.

Kull, Steven, Clay Ramsay, and Evan Lewis. 2003. Misperceptions, the media, and the Iraq war. *Political Science Quarterly* 118, 4: 569–599.

Lessig, Lawrence. 2004. *Free Culture: How Big Media Uses Technology and the Law to Lock Down Culture and Control Creativity*. London, UK: Penguin Press.

———. 2006. *Code: Version 2.0*. New York, NY: Basic Books.

Manovich, Lev. 2002. *The Language of New Media*. Cambridge, MA: MIT Press.

McLuhan, Marshall, and Lewis H. Lapham. 1994. *Understanding Media: The Extensions of Man*. Cambridge, MA: MIT Press.

Merrin, William. 2005. *Baudrillard and the Media*. London, UK: Polity Press.

Monge, Peter R., and Noshir Contractor. 2003. *Theories of Communication Networks*. New York, NY: Oxford University Press.

Neff, Gina. 2011. *Venture Labor*. Cambridge, MA: MIT Press.

Neff, Gina and David Stark. 2004. Permanently Beta: Responsive Organization in the Internet Era. In *Society Online: The Internet in Context*, ed. Philip N. Howard and Steve Jones. Thousand Oaks, CA: Sage Press.

Pew Internet and American Life Project. 2005. Data Memo: Filesharing. www.pewinternet.org.

———. 2008. Data Memo: The internet and the 2008 election. www.pewinternet.org.

Pew Research Center for the People and the Press. 2007. Data Memo: Public knowledge of current affairs little changed by news and information revolutions. www.people-press.org.

Poulantzas, Nicos, and Patrick Camiller. 2001. *State, Power, Socialism*. London, UK: Verso.

Project for Excellence in Journalism. 2007. The state of the news media 2007. http://www.stateofthemedia.org/2007/.

Putnam, Robert D. 2001. *Bowling Alone: The Collapse and Revival of American Community*. New York, NY: Simon & Schuster.

Rheingold, Howard. 2000. *The Virtual Community: Homesteading on the Electronic Frontier*. Cambridge, MA: MIT Press.

———. 2002. *Smart Mobs: The Next Social Revolution*. New York, NY: Basic Books.

Sassen, Saskia. 2001. *The Global City: New York, London, Tokyo*. Princeton, NJ: Princeton University Press.

————. 2006. *Territory, Authority, Rights: From Medieval to Global Assemblages*. Princeton, NJ: Princeton University Press.

Saxenian, AnnaLee. 1996. *Regional Advantage: Culture and Competition in Silicon Valley and Route 128*. Cambridge, MA: Harvard University Press.

Solomon, Deborah. 2010. Sex and the single man. *New York Times Magazine*, July 5.

Stalder, Felix. 2006. *Manuel Castells: the Theory of the Network Society*. Cambridge, UK: Polity.

Stohl, Cynthia, and Michael Stohl. 2007. Networks of terror: Theoretical assumptions and pragmatic consequences. *Communication Theory* 17, 2: 93–124.

Stromer-Galley, Jennifer. 2000. Online interaction and why candidates avoid it. *Journal of Communication* 50, 4: 111–132.

Suchman, Lucy. 2006. *Human-Machine Reconfigurations: Plans and Situated Actions*. 2nd edn. Cambridge, UK: Cambridge University Press.

Susser, Ida. 2002. *The Castells Reader on Cities and Social Theory*. New York, NY: Wiley-Blackwell.

Turner, Fred. 2006. *From Counterculture to Cyberculture: Stewart Brand, the Whole Earth Network, and the Rise of Digital Utopianism*. Chicago, IL: University of Chicago Press.

van Dijk, Jan. 2006. *The Network Society: Social Aspects of New Media*. Thousand Oaks, CA: Sage.

von Hippel, Eric. 2005. *Democratizing Innovation*. Cambridge, MA: MIT Press.

GLOSSARY/INDEX